Capturing Mood
in Watercolor

Phil Austin

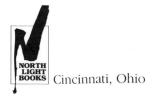
NORTH LIGHT BOOKS Cincinnati, Ohio

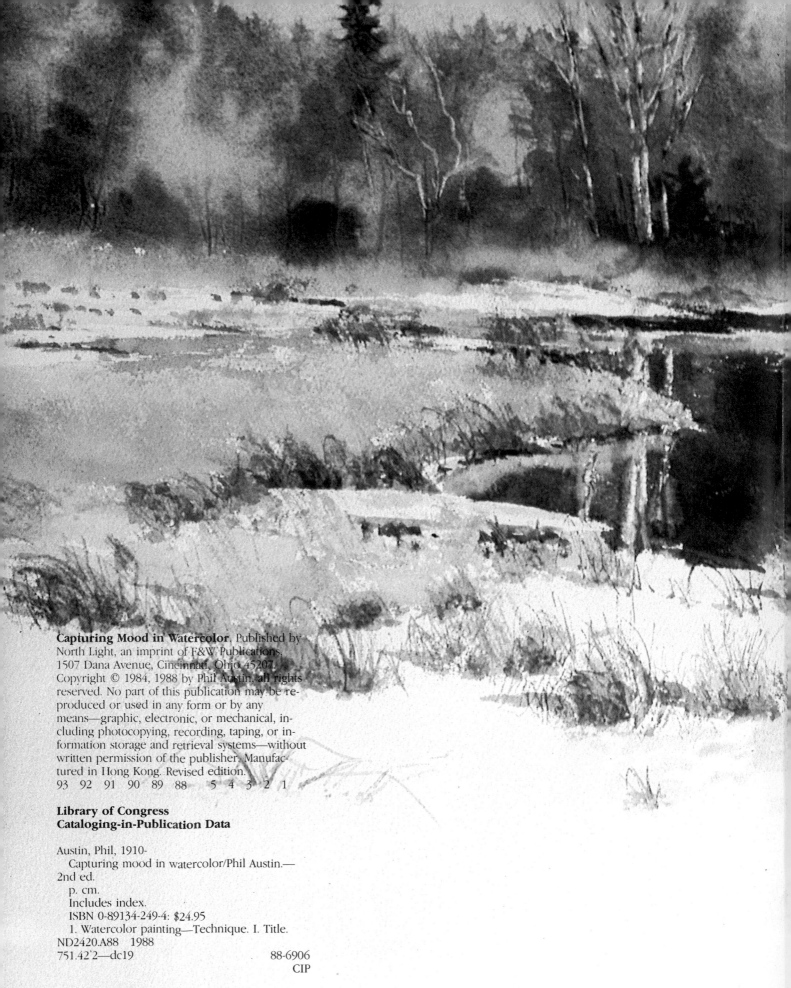

Capturing Mood in Watercolor. Published by
North Light, an imprint of F&W Publications,
1507 Dana Avenue, Cincinnati, Ohio 45207.
Copyright © 1984, 1988 by Phil Austin, all rights
reserved. No part of this publication may be re-
produced or used in any form or by any
means—graphic, electronic, or mechanical, including photocopying, recording, taping, or information storage and retrieval systems—without
written permission of the publisher. Manufac-
tured in Hong Kong. Revised edition.
93 92 91 90 89 88   5 4 3 2 1

**Library of Congress
Cataloging-in-Publication Data**

Austin, Phil, 1910-
    Capturing mood in watercolor/Phil Austin.—
2nd ed.
    p. cm.
    Includes index.
    ISBN 0-89134-249-4: $24.95
    1. Watercolor painting—Technique. I. Title.
ND2420.A88 1988
751.42'2—dc19   88-6906
                                        CIP

Editor: Linda Sanders
Designer: Carol Buchanan

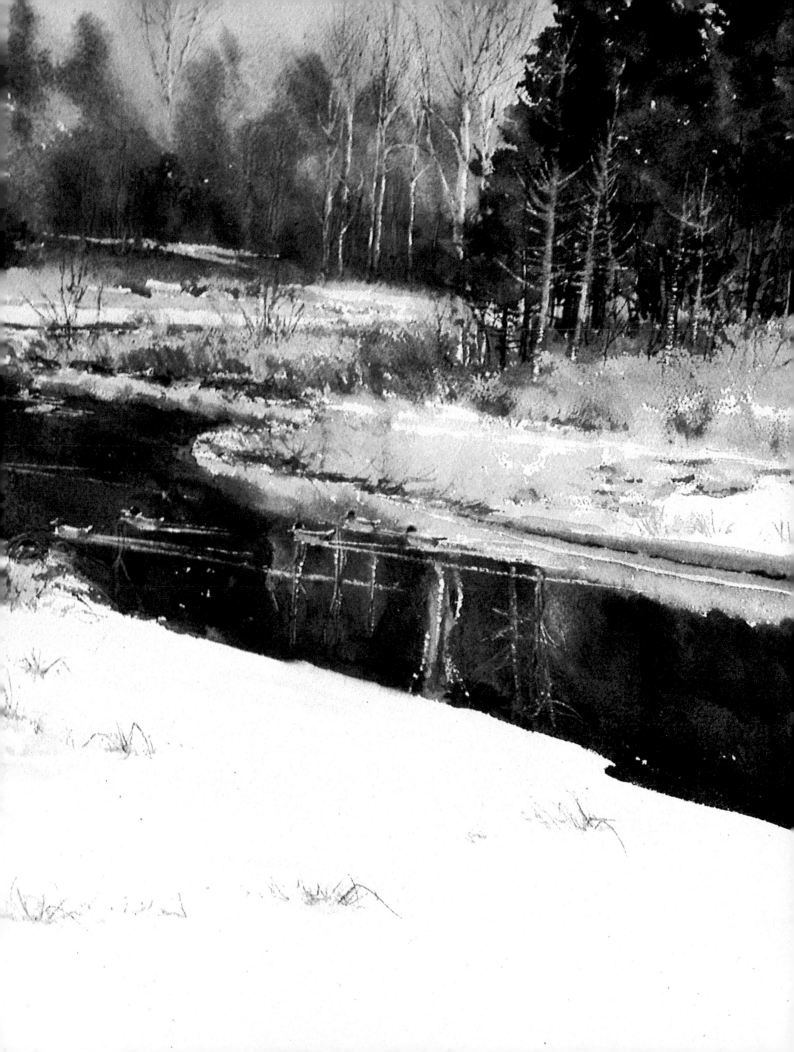

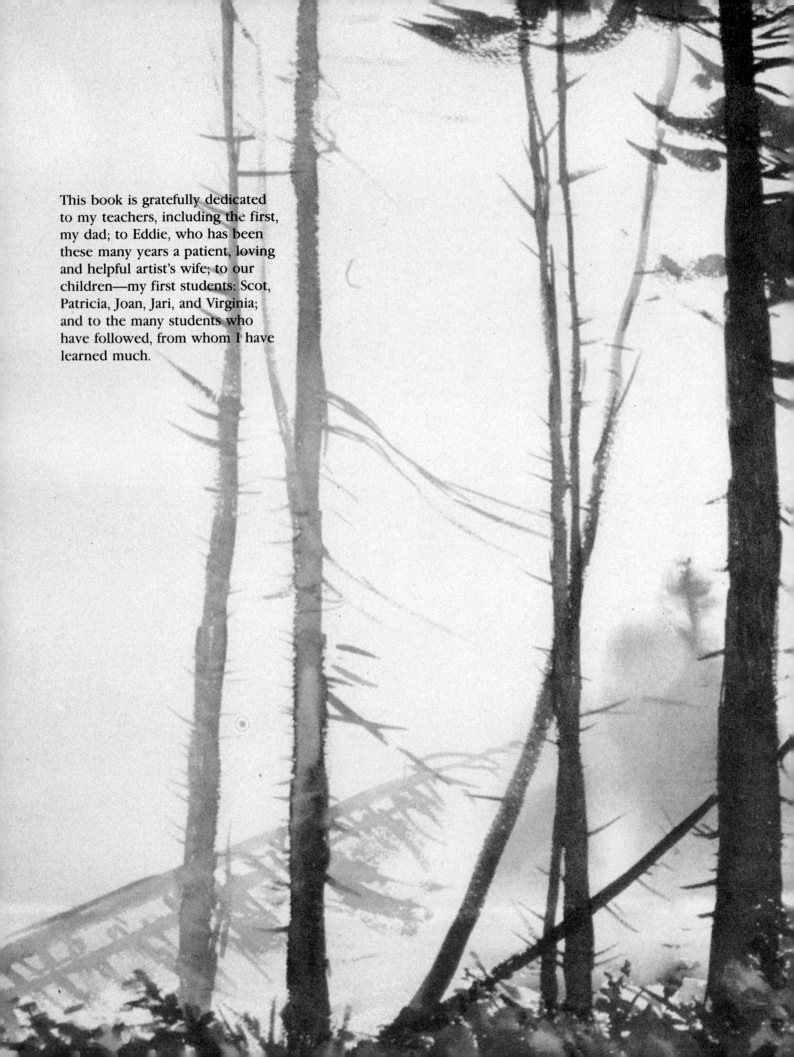

This book is gratefully dedicated
to my teachers, including the first,
my dad; to Eddie, who has been
these many years a patient, loving
and helpful artist's wife; to our
children—my first students: Scot,
Patricia, Joan, Jari, and Virginia;
and to the many students who
have followed, from whom I have
learned much.

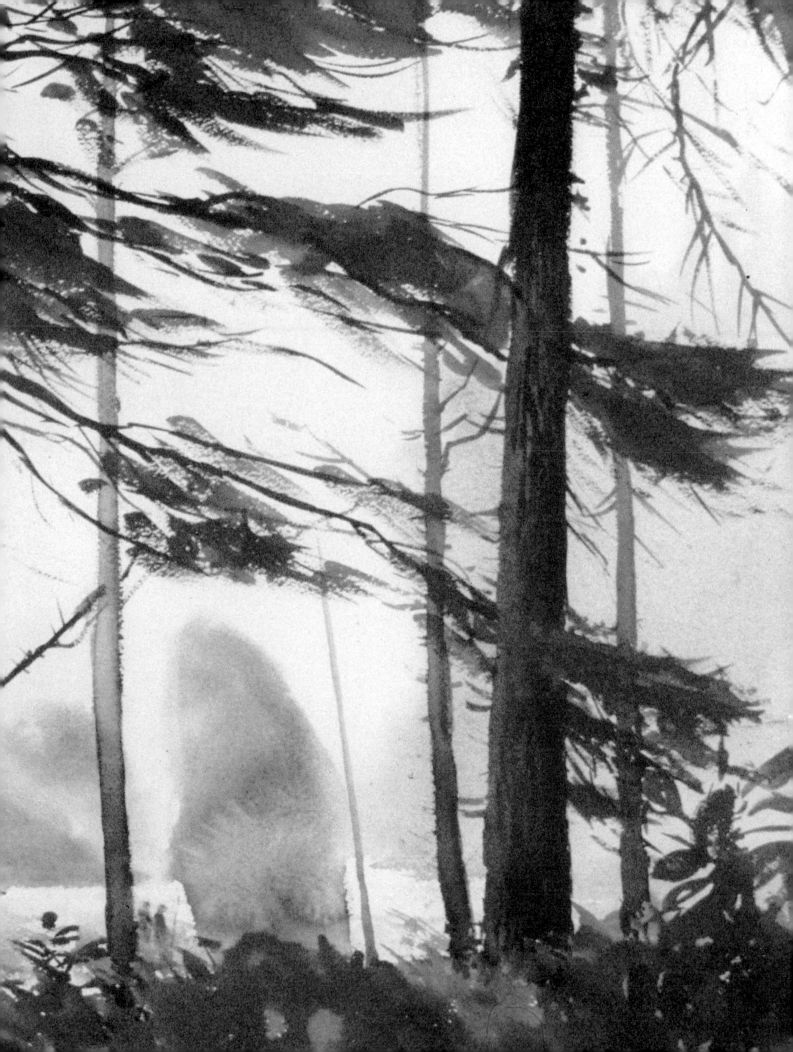

Contents

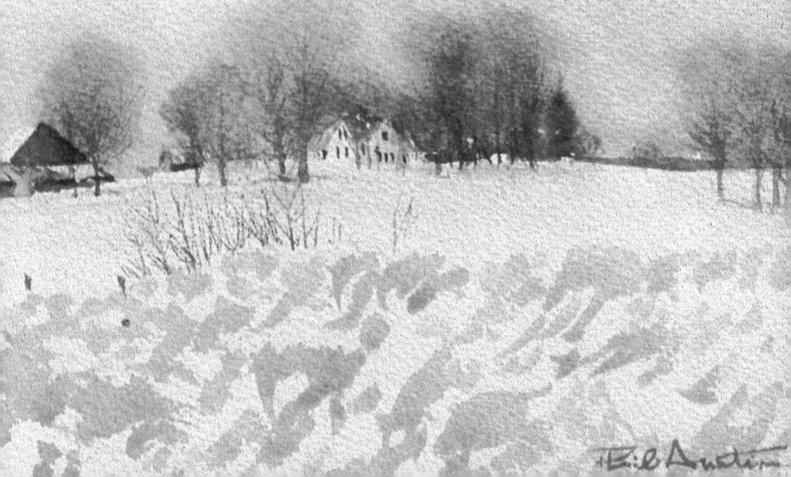

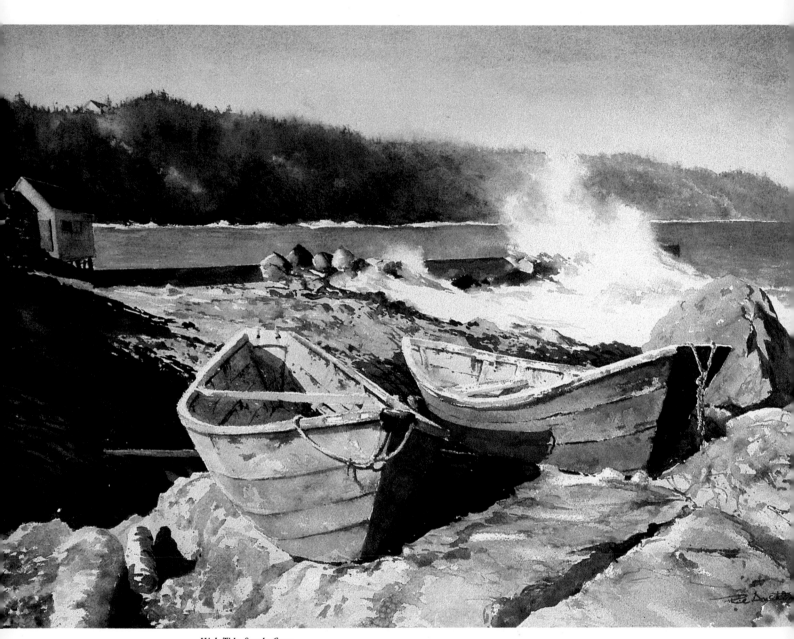

High Tide, Sandy Cove,
Nova Scotia
21 × 29 inches

Foreword

In today's world there is a strong inclination to remain in our own small niche, the idea being that if we become "involved," we make ourselves vulnerable. We live in an apartment building or on a quiet street and fail to get acquainted with our neighbors. If we make acquaintances, we never get involved in personal conversation. We don't express our opinions lest someone disagree with us. We don't voice our deepest feelings for fear we may be ridiculed.

In spite of living in this kind of restrictive climate, many individuals still feel compelled to express themselves. Some write letters to the editor; others champion a cause; some write articles, books, or poetry; others act or compose music. And some create objects of art.

Having done a large number of watercolor workshops, I have found that people paint for numerous and varied reasons. Some are seeking relaxation—complete absorption in a field widely separated from their daily occupation. Others have found that painting increases their awareness of the world around them. What a pleasure it is for me to travel with a group and after a week of painting note their greater appreciation of the landscape on the trip back home than they showed on the outbound trip. Still others are looking for a means of expressing their interpretation of what they see about them. Many are seeking personal satisfaction through a sense of accomplishment by developing an individual skill.

Many of the ideas set forth in this book are not new or original with me, but time has shown they offer the serious student a better use of watercolor as a painting medium. Many of the procedures will apply equally well to any means of picture making, although they have been set down with watercolor painting in mind.

I have tried to set forth in simple terms and demonstrations the way I think and work. Whether you are already an accomplished painter, an advanced amateur, or even a hopeful beginner, watercolor is an "open end" medium. There exists no level of accomplishment beyond which the painter cannot go.

This book has been written with the hope that it will aid all who seek help. If it shares with you my enthusiasm for watercolor painting, the joy of spontaneous creation that comes with watercolor, and the emotional release of telling the story of the beautiful world we have about us, then my purpose has been accomplished.

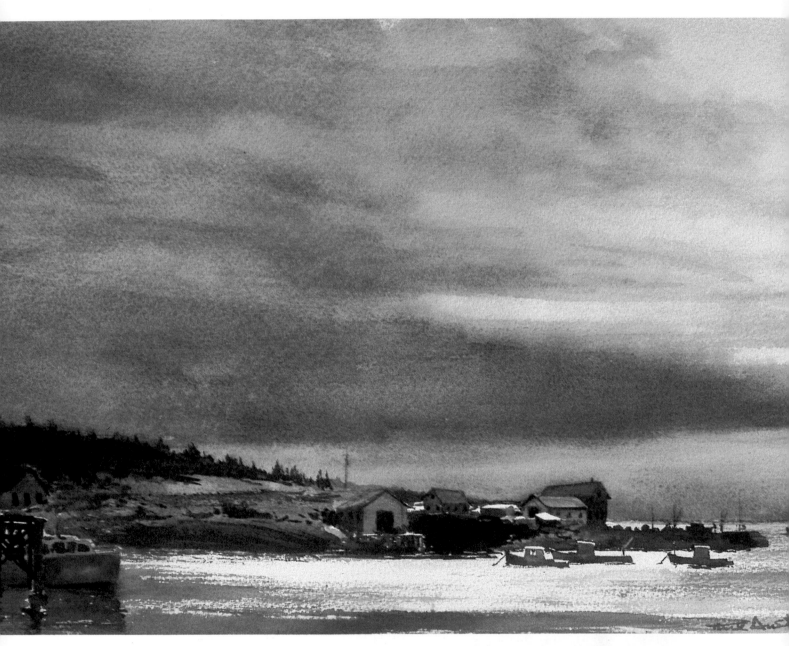

Evening at Indian Harbour
11½ × 15⅝ inches

The moody sky and reflected light on the water help capture a sense of this Nova Scotia harbor town. A simple pattern of lights and darks helps pull the small objects into a very effective composition.

Introduction

MEET THE ARTIST

There are many ways of storytelling. Some do it with a marvelous command of words. Some choose music, while others paint. Regardless of the medium, all are ways of manifesting emotional expression.

I constantly drew pictures, as children do, and the gift of a small box of brushes and paints ushered me into the joyous world of painting. Things that interested me and stirred my emotions prompted the desire to express them in paintings. The far-off whistle of a night freight carried on the wind, or the sight of wooded hills and rolling fields drifting in the blue haze of autumn brought wanderlust, yet demanded more than just exploring the beyond.

When I was very young we lived on a small farm at the fringe of a Lake Michigan harbor town. The deep-throated call of the lake freighters nosing into the harbor brought a desire to interpret that excitement in a painting. One night when we visited the slip where a freighter was moored to unload coal, lights blinked everywhere, conveyors clattered, the deck lights seemed as high as the sky and glimmered into the darkness for a mile! My enchantment was complete and my interest in working boats was born. Life was nudging me to paint.

With a dad who was sensitive to my moods

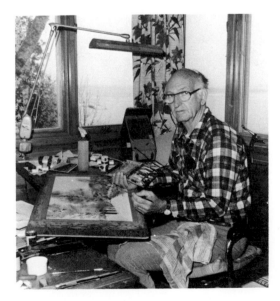

The author in his studio.

and interests, I sketched the river bank: bushes, boulders, deep pools, and eddies. I scanned the countryside from the hilltops, and studied shadows on country roads. All became entangled with my dreams and desires. So began the training of a storyteller.

FORMAL TRAINING

I attended the University of Michigan because excellent art classes were available in the architectural school. My excitement about the courses and love of the atmosphere of the art school gave me thorough enjoyment and exposure to the art world. At that time watercolor painting was introduced to me. The ease with which some of the students flowed their colors and achieved satisfying results made me envious and frustrated, but my early discouragement was offset by a growing love for the medium and a determination to master it.

Frequent visits to the excellent school art library brought me an awareness of many great painters, including Constable, Inness, Turner, the French Impressionists, the American painters—Homer, Burchfield, Hopper, Marin—and the current watercolorists Whorf and Heitland. One book which I constantly returned to was a fine volume with many superb plates of the works of the British painter, Russell Flint. His mastery of beautiful washes still amazes me. A few years later it was possible to study some of the work of many of these artists firsthand in Chicago galleries and at the Annual International Watercolor Exhibition, held at the Chicago Art Institute. About this time I also began to see and admire the work of Andrew Wyeth.

At the university our painting classes followed the pattern (much disliked by many students today) of working from a carefully planned still life. There was much validity in this method of learning. The objects that emerged from the property cabinets were endless—simple sculpture, beautiful plates, bowls and vases, background drapes, bottles in all shapes, sizes, and colors. Plants, fresh fruits, and flowers were often added. Thus we were introduced to the challenge of capturing textures, form, colors, light, and shadow—compositions under a constant light source—and were not confused by changing conditions, which could have easily happened since we were beginners.

Two of these early still lifes remain in my

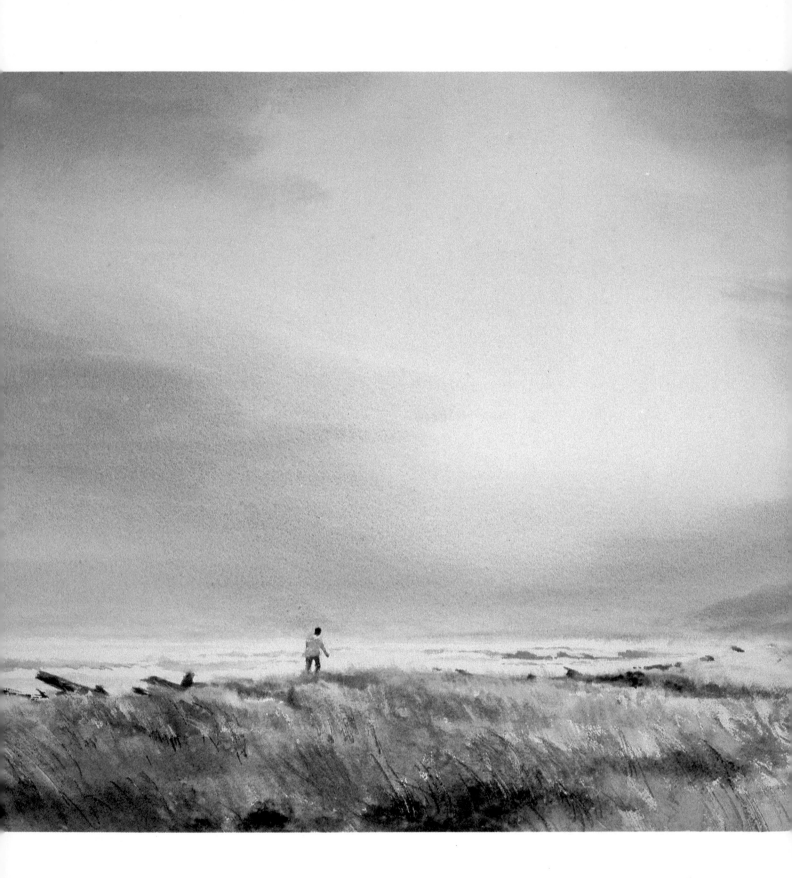

mind for specific reasons. One contained a clay pot of "hen and chicken" cactus. Its complexity taught me to work wet and strive for an interpretation rather than a painstaking rendering. The other subject was an Indian pottery with a brilliantly colored serape. I became aware of the simplicity of the rich, earth-colored pottery against the play of bright color and painted with new purpose. I learned that it was better to express feelings about a subject than to play the part of a camera.

A PAINTING CAREER

Further study in night classes at the American Academy of Art in Chicago followed. I worked for several years in a large commercial art studio in the city and even though I enjoyed the work, I yearned for a painting career. Freelancing followed, and I was allowed more time for painting. Those years were valuable, a good discipline, and gradually brought me to the point of "taking the plunge" into full-time painting.

I have devoted my entire energy to painting for some twenty years now. It has been a most satisfying life. Being a workshop instructor in recent years has taught me a great deal, while I have sought to help others. In the pages that follow, I'd like to share my enthusiasm for the joy of expression in watercolor and the methods effective in achieving these goals.

Pacific Solitude
21 × 29 inches
Collection of Mrs. Phil Austin

This self-portrait was a response to my love for the sea beaches. It was done wet-on-wet and the beach grass was dry-brushed into a damp surface. Limited brush-handle work was also done while the painting was still damp, as were some changes in value and color. When the painting was dry, a few details, including the hiker (who is me), were added.

PAINTING AS AN EMOTIONAL RESPONSE

The wonder of life is the immeasurable beauty in the small area of the universe with which we are acquainted. Even more amazing is the fact that our Creator has made each of us capable of experiencing an individual emotional response to what goes on about us. I believe that the nebulous gift called "talent" is the degree of our emotional response. The stronger that response, the more likely we are to create something tangible, be it prose, poetry, music, sculpture, or paintings.

It may never be our privilege to personally realize the impact of that revelation on others. But by whatever means, our expression must be completely honest. It will be an exposure of our innermost selves. Our work will be *us*.

Living in the country the majority of my formative years, I developed a genuine love for the out-of-doors and turned naturally to painting landscape. Awareness of so much beauty prompted a desire to capture on paper those qualities that are so often momentary.

This raises the question of whether talent is an innate ability or a genuine love for a particular pursuit. At least one of the chief ingredients of talent is surely the love that puts a certain endeavor in the forefront of one's activities.

A natural ease for drawing or painting without love for it accomplishes little. An acquaintance once said to me, "I really enjoy doing watercolors. If I had the time I'm sure I could do some really good ones." When asked what kept him from taking the time needed, he replied that his sailboat required a lot of work every spring and that, of course, in the summer he liked to spend most of his spare time on the water. His talent was water, not watercolor.

Painting, like any other skill, makes real demands on our time if we are serious about it.

As artists, we have a responsibility to create awareness in others. It takes a great deal of searching and practice to translate emotions into visual images. How shall we reveal the incredible beauty of nature in its uncountable aspects? Or how will we show the beauty man has incorporated into the objects he has created for daily use? Sometimes remnants of the past stir more emotion than the substance of our present lives. These challenges make watercolor an exciting search.

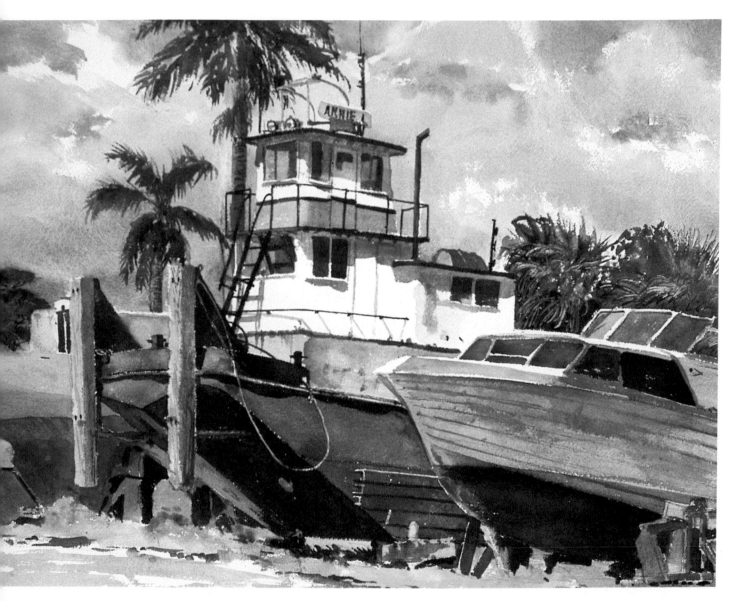

Florida Potpourri
21½ × 29 inches

The transparent qualities of watercolor—making use of the brightness of the white paper—were perfect for capturing this old river tug towering over the surrounding boats. I made some changes, some simplification, moved the palm trees a bit in the interest of a better composition, and hastened to capture it on a sheet of Arches rough.

1. Choosing and Using Your Materials

WHY WATERCOLOR?

Watercolor is ideally suited to expressing the emotions and moods nature inspires. It is flexible, fluid, and subtle. It invites spontaneity. And because its results are often unpredictable it can be full of surprises. You may complete a painting and find effects you did not consciously strive for. I believe that God helps us to exceed our humble ability, whatever we are doing. This is especially true in painting with watercolor, and it adds joy to the experience.

Watercolor may become your overwhelming choice, as with me. I think it is the most exciting, the most versatile, the most expressive, and perhaps the most baffling medium of all.

VERSATILITY OF WATERCOLOR

Because watercolor is such a versatile medium it can become, more than any other medium, an incentive to have fun when you paint. It will lend itself readily to a vast variety of subject material. With practice and an increasing ability to handle watercolor comes the urge to tackle more and more diverse subject material. You may be challenged by the seacoast, as well as rapids and waterfalls. You may find it fun to incorporate deer, foxes, horses, and cows into your works and then enjoy going to sketch class to paint figures and even portraits in watercolor.

The discipline of using watercolor simply sharpens one's observation and forces direct work. Practice in a sketch class makes it much easier and more fun to add figures when needed in a painting. Simple quick sketches will help you master painting water, trees, or skies.

If you lean toward being a documentary painter, you will have fun doing such subjects as the old rusty lantern in "Emma's Lantern," a rock outcrop, the end of a stone wall draped with snow, or a section of an old building.

As a watercolor enthusiast, you will eagerly search to find the best way to tell the softness of tawny meadow grass blowing in the wind, the fresh, pale beauty of the yellow-green smoke of spring willows against the darker backdrop of woods, the rugged individuality of old gnarled and twisted trees, the silver of water shimmering in the morning light, the sparkle of a brook picking its way over rocks and stones between dark banks of earth and

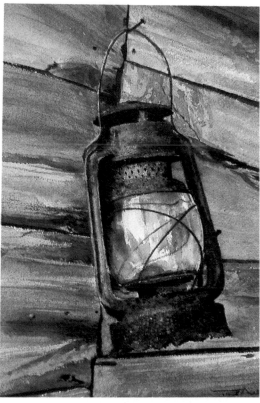

Emma's Lantern
15⅝ × 11¾ inches

Because watercolor is so versatile, it can also be used for subjects like this rusty old lantern. It was painted with a charged wash of ultramarine and vermilion. Table salt was then dropped into the wash to create the effect of rust as the values were molded. A little cerulean added here and there gives a hint of the color when new. Old weathered boards further suggest age.

the vast changing mass of clouds creating an endless landscape in the sky. For all of this, watercolor has much to offer.

The more your initial washes imply by directness and simplicity—by direction of stroke, texture, change of value, choice of color, looseness of application, emotional expression and elimination of unnecessary detail—the better your painting will become.

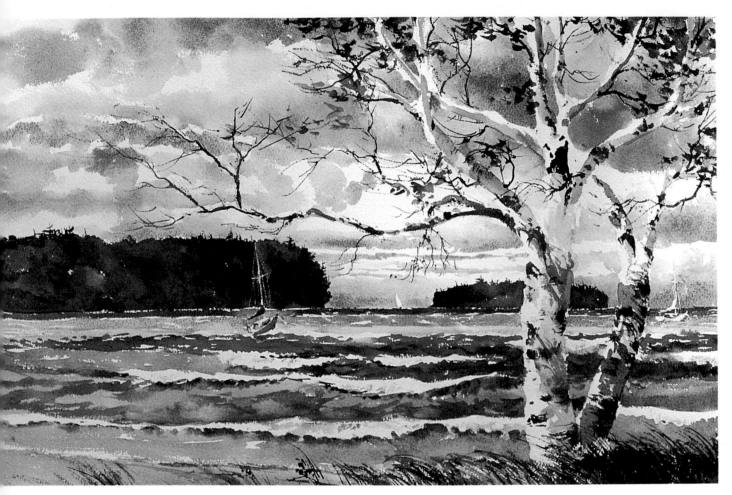

Wind at Ephraim
14 × 21 inches

Painting on location can help you capture mood more accurately. The wind fairly rocked the car as I painted this scene, so I suggested wind with the broken sky and the anchored sailboat rearing at its mooring in the middle distance. I used the turmoil of the strokes to suggest sound as well. Lots of white paper was left for curling spray, light on the birch, and the passage of clouds.

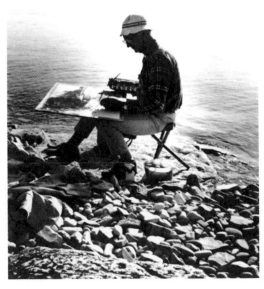

Sitting on a comfortable stool, water bucket nearby, paper on a board across the knees, paint box securely in hand, makes it easy to work outdoors. The board can be tilted in any direction to control the wash. Being near the ground makes other tools easily accessible.

October Reflections
21¹/₂ × 29 inches

8

GOING OUT TO PAINT OR BRINGING THE OUT-OF-DOORS IN

Painting on location can be a rewarding experience. It sharpens observation and teaches selectivity, and it can result in a mental bank of useful information and detail. Working on location will make you a part of what is going on so you'll paint with more understanding.

Most of this painting came from my imagination, so it didn't matter whether I painted it on location or in the studio. Note the subject material from which the painting was created, shown at right.

The sky was painted after *the trees—which allowed me to leave little sparkles of white paper around the leaves and trunks of the birches, as well as the maples. Even the distant evergreens have bits of this sparkle, since the water was painted* after *these trees.*

For many years I painted entirely out-of-doors. Eventually, by taking photo slides of my painting subjects, I was able to increase my source material, which resulted in more creativity back in the home studio. Studio painting then became a great experience with more op-

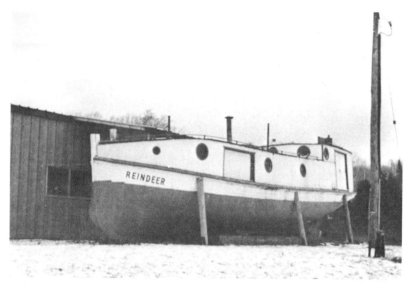

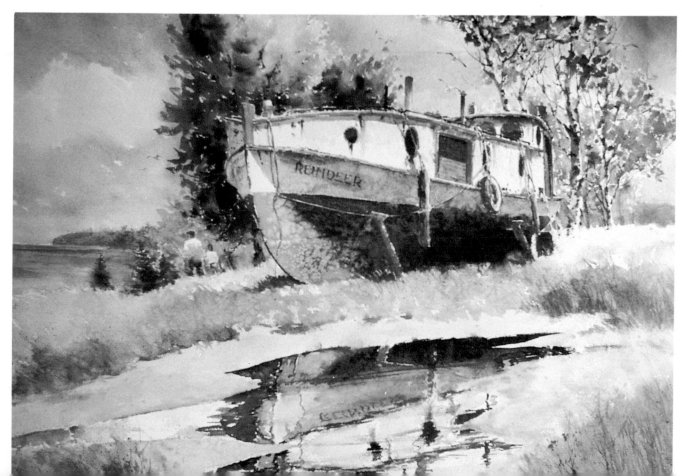

portunity for study and experiment, based on what was learned on location.

Many things often interfere with painting out-of-doors. Time may be limited, at times even a place to sit and work is virtually impossible to find, or the weather may be prohibitory. However, trying to paint from slides or photos without enough prior painting on location to get the "feel" of the area, the color, and the activity taking place is futile. Try to imagine doing a portrait of a person from random snapshots which capture a passing mood entirely unlike the person, and you'll know what I mean. Photos are valuable as reference material and should be treated as such, not as pictures to be copied.

PAINTING ON LOCATION

If you plan to go very far on foot to reach a painting location you will soon learn to scale down the amount of gear you choose to carry. A couple of bad falls while overloaded without a free hand to catch myself discouraged me from carrying more than the absolute essentials. I now carry a fairly lightweight plywood board with my paper taped to it, a simple collapsible stool, a plastic water bucket large enough to hold a gallon jug of water, and a simple shoulder strap case for paints, brushes, paint rag, pencils, erasers, a spray bottle, sketch book, my camera, and some *insect spray*. This last item is often a necessity!

Since an easel is a bulky extra, the habit of sitting on a stool with your board across your knees may prove helpful. Never gamble on finding water when you are taking a long hike to paint! I hiked through the woods and brush out to the coast in Washington state once, only to end up with a fantastic beach subject two hundred feet below and no access to water!

The case I carry is a simple leather one which can be made by a local leather craftsman. It is 7″ × 13″ × 16″ deep and accommodates a large, discarded cardboard soap box which fits perfectly and stiffens the case. There is extra space around the side for two 12″ × 16″ watercolor blocks. (I carry a cold-press and a rough block with me for additional painting or sketching.) There is also room for a 6″ × 8½″ sketch book, an extra large wash brush or two, and a roll of tape.

You may find it valuable on extra bright days to take along a light nylon beach umbrella

with a sectional aluminum-spiked shaft to shade your painting surface.

PAINTING IN THE STUDIO

If you plan to paint regularly at home you will want to arrange some permanent work space so that everything doesn't have to be dragged out and put away every time you wish to paint. If you are fortunate enough to have a spare room with north light it should make an ideal painting space. You will also need suitable work space for matting and framing, and storage space for mat boards, watercolor paper, reference material, and books, as well as a place to keep all gear for outdoor sketching and painting. Go to a good art supply store and discuss the type of artificial light best for painting. Either the proper balance of fluorescent bulbs or a combination of fluorescent and incandescent lighting should be considered.

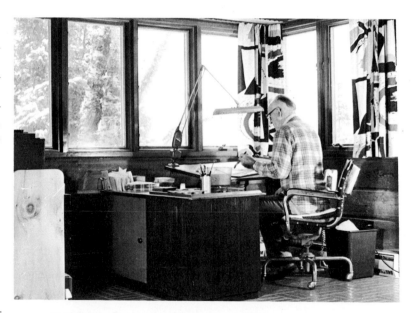

My well-lighted, pleasant painting area. The silk-screened drapery material with a colorful pattern of brush strokes was a real "find."

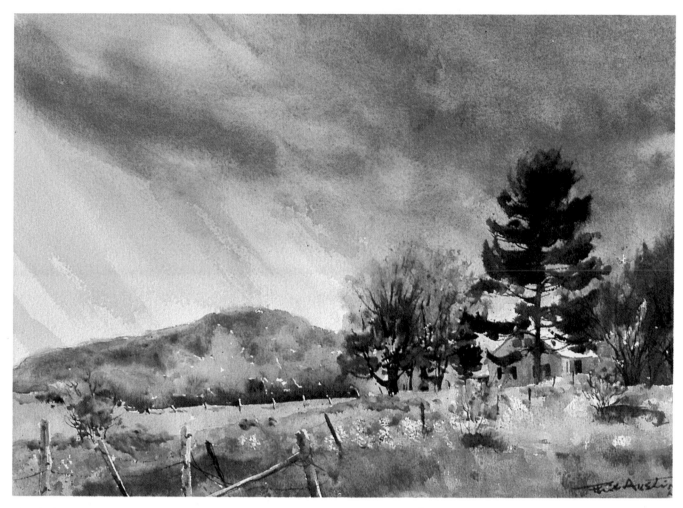

This little watercolor was done very fast and direct with a variety of greens and values, easily achieved with the limited palette. The gray storm cloud and the rain-streaked sky were put in wet.

Afternoon Shower
11½ × 15⅝ inches

MATERIALS

Materials are very much a matter of individual preference. However, there are some basic rules to follow in choosing them. Whatever your way of working, except for purely practice sketches, it is wise to use good materials. A little care in selecting pigments, for example, will insure using non-fugitive colors—a must if you plan to sell your work. Look on the color chart of whatever brand you choose and check the permanency rating given each color. It is a great disappointment to have created an exciting watercolor, only to discover later on that one or more of the colors are beginning to fade in the light. Brands may vary somewhat in the characteristics of particular colors. It is wise to settle on a brand you like and then always use the same pigments. The consistency will help your painting. Having begun with Winsor & Newton's, after a little experiment-ing with other brands, I have continued with them through the years, now using their "se-lected list" pigments in the large tubes.

THE LIMITED PALETTE

To simplify procedure and get direct results I recommend limiting the number of colors on your palette. They should be colors that mix equally well with others in either direction of the spectrum without turning muddy, that produce rich darks without the use of black, and that are nonstaining and permanent. The following seven colors compose a palette that meets these requirements. With practice and experience you may want to make substitu-tions or additions, but be sure your choices meet with the criteria just mentioned.

Alizarin Crimson
Vermilion
Cadmium Orange
Cadmium Yellow Pale (or tint)
Viridian
Ultramarine (or French Ultramarine)
Cerulean Blue

Learning to use seven or eight colors is much easier than learning to use twenty-five or thirty. Knowing the properties and characteristics of individual colors has a lot to do with how well you can use them. Some will float, others will mix readily, others will create a grainy wash—all characteristics that you can utilize to good advantage in creating various textures and visual effects.

Using a limited palette means constant mixing of color, which will teach color appreciation and sensitivity to subtle changes in color and value; thus sharpening our appreciation of what we see. The limited palette I prescribe is actually composed of the primaries—red, yellow, and blue—plus the secondaries—orange, green, and in place of purple alizarin crimson, a more versatile substitute for purple. It includes a second blue—cerulean—which greatly expands the range of blues. By the choice of hue of each color and by working transparently on white paper, the watercolor painter comes close to demonstrating the way colors behave when separated out of light by a prism.

I'll provide more information on mixing colors with the limited palette in Chapter 6.

PAPER

As to papers, the important thing is to use 100 percent rag paper for your serious work so that your paper, like your color, will be permanent. One-hundred-forty-pound is a good weight to use, but it should be stretched to make it flat. If you go to 300-pound stock you will only need to make stretches for the wettest paintings. The heavier paper is much more apt to lie flat under the mat when framed. Handmade papers give a wonderful quality to a painting. Some are hard to find. There are, however, a number of good papers available. I like Arches paper. For smaller paintings their 12"x16" blocks in cold-press and rough are good. For half sheets and larger you will want to stretch 140-pound paper or use 300-pound.

Working methods, and sometimes the subjects themselves, will determine whether you wish to use a rough, cold-press, or hot-press paper. I generally prefer rough or occasionally cold press for most of my work. If you plan to use lift-off methods to remove limited color, you may prefer smoother papers. The important thing is always to use good rag papers for

anything but practice work. Cheaper papers tend to discolor in time.

STRETCHING PROCEDURE

A good stretching procedure: Soak the paper briefly in the tub or shower and spread it on a piece of 3/8-inch plywood and tape it down securely with 1 or 1½-inch paper packaging tape. To avoid trouble with this tape coming loose, remove moisture ½ to ¾ of an inch from the edge of the paper with facial tissue or a paper towel so that the glue on the tape remains full strength. Moistening the tape by drawing it across a wet sponge will also avoid washing glue off the tape and will help insure a good stretch. As a further precaution, use a flat object and squeegee the tape tightly to the paper as it is applied. Most stretches break loose because glue has been washed off the tape or because the tape has not been pressed tightly enough to remove excess air—particularly with rougher papers. Once your stretch is made, allow it to dry in a flat position, not standing on edge, as this allows water to accumulate at one side of the sheet, again loosening the stretch.

BRUSHES

Brushes also are a matter of personal preference. I like sables even though they're more expensive and use a number of flats from 1/8 to 3/4-inch wide—plus some no. 2 and no. 4 round sables. Occasionally a no. 14 round is helpful. Two or three large wash brushes, a 1¼, 1½ and 2 inch, plus a no. 3 and a no. 6 rigger for doing branches, ship's lines, and such, and a 3/4 inch aquarelle for texture and "brush handle" work will prove valuable. Some of the new white sable flats are also good to have. (You perhaps will want a slender painting knife for some scraping out.)

PALETTES

There are a number of good palettes available. I prefer a lightweight aluminum box palette, made by Winsor & Newton, which has a white interior with small wells for color, larger mixing areas, and a thumb ring on the bottom, making it easy to hold when painting on location. (Especially helpful if there is much wind!) For a limited palette of seven colors, this works well and can be supplemented with an ordinary muffin tin, which has larger cups in which to mix color for extensive areas of wash. In the studio it is also helpful to use a plastic palette with large mixing areas.

SKETCH BOOK

A bound sketch book of smooth paper (either 8½"x11" or smaller) is a necessity, together with a supply of soft pencils, such as no. 2 office pencils or "B" or "2B" drawing pencils, and kneaded erasers. These allow for recording details on location and working out composition by experimenting with thumbnail sketches.

Winter on Rt. 57
21½ × 29 inches

MISCELLANEOUS

A liquid mask is good for occasional use. Choose one of the thin varieties, which handle much like watercolor.

A painting apron is helpful if you are inclined to slop color around freely. A towel across your knees will help for occasional wiping of the brush or for drying it slightly, since the use of a towel rather than frequent washing or flipping of the brush will avoid an unconscious waste of a lot of valuable pigment.

Two other items are a spray bottle with an adjustable nozzle, and a high speed electric dryer for studio use. The dryer will allow you to dry areas either to arrest action of the color at a desired point or to speed up your painting procedure.

You might also want to have handy table salt, to be used in creating some textures; a sponge for drying areas of the paper; and a proportion wheel, to be used when transferring the initial sketch to the painting surface.

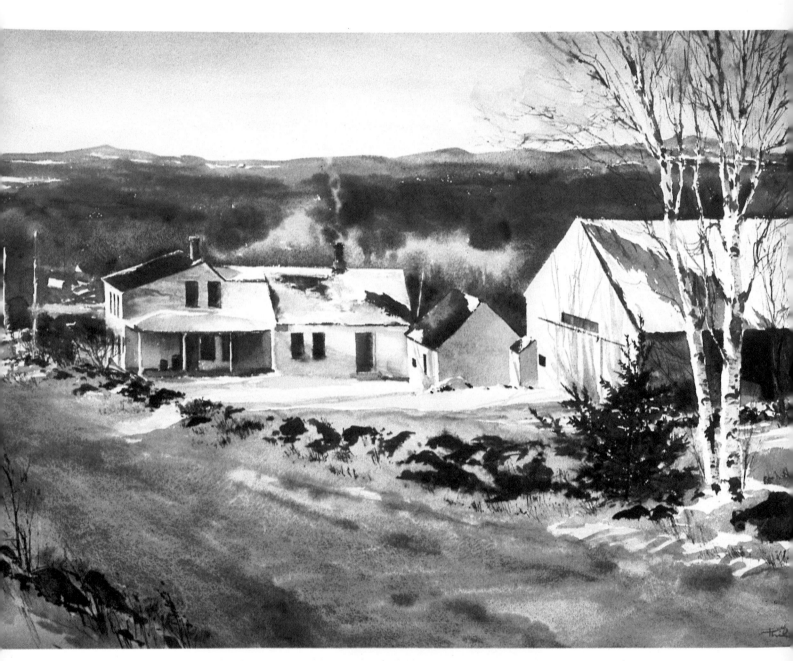

Farm on Catamount Mountain
21×29 inches

Careful planning helped capture the subdued mood of late afternoon in this painting. The snowy road leads your eye to the center of interest, which is spotlighted in sun against the dark, wooded hills in the distance. The birch on the right bridges the foreground, middle ground, and background. Contrast is emphasized at building corners, and horizontal shadows establish middle distance. All these decisions must be made before any paint is applied.

2. Planning Your Picture

The old saying, "You can't change horses in the middle of the stream," must have been originated by a watercolor painter. Once you are committed on a watercolor, there is seldom time or opportunity to stop, debate, or change your original plan. For that reason, it is necessary to make adequate preparation. A mental review is helpful. Ask yourself: What is my interest in the subject? What is it that I want to paint? Why do I want to paint it? Does it need to be painted? Does it stir an emotional response in me? What kind of mood does it generate? If it has been done before, have I something new to say? Does it really need to be painted again? What do I particularly like about it? What am I going to emphasize? What things will I need to change? Am I excited enough about it? Will the final result be worth the time and effort?

When these decisions are reached, you need to give serious thought to the basics of composition, a must for producing a good painting.

The mood you want the painting to convey is one of the first considerations in planning your painting. Composition and mood are closely related, although the effect of composition on the painting's mood is sometimes very subtle.

For example, the use of strong verticals will create an alert or forceful sensation, whereas horizontal space can help express calm or soothing emotion. The longer and narrower the space, the stronger the feeling of power.

Composition must work with other factors if it is to express mood effectively. For instance, if the colors used are harmonious with little change in value, the shapes within the painting will need to be larger and simpler. Expressing forceful emotion requires strong contrasts and contrasting movement, perhaps even sharp angular areas, rather than flowing, undulating shapes. An excellent example would be a painting of the Rocky Mountains with sharp peaks, hard edges, and extreme light areas contrasting with deep shadows. On the other hand, a painting of an area such as the Smokies in eastern Tennessee that conveys a gentler mood would involve areas of soft haze, flowing hills, and gradual changes in value. Any strong contrast would need to be small in area, drawing interest perhaps, but not dominating the landscape.

SEARCHING FOR SUBJECT MATTER

When you are "prowling" a new area in the car and see a likely spot, try to find a suitable pull-out where you can park and study things more fully. As you move on, look in the rearview mirror. You may discover a whole new perspective behind you.

Sometimes it also pays to turn around and go back for a second look. How many times when something along the road seemed to have great possibilities, have you driven on, promising that undoubtedly there would be something as good or better ahead, or that you could always return? Many times I've regretted such a decision. Once, however, while driving through southern Indiana, I passed a marvel-

November Washday
21¹/₂ × 29¹/₂ inches

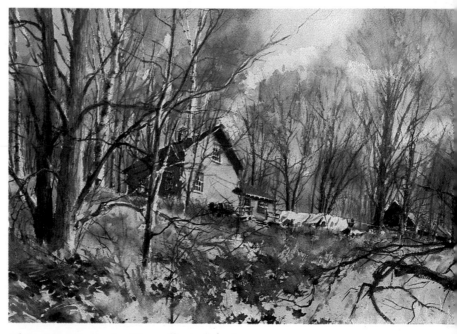

Planning my composition allowed me to make one significant change in this scene. The simple house sitting in a corner woodlot has a special appeal for me; I've painted it in different seasons and weather. But this time I decided to put in a line of fresh washing together with a laundress to add interest and connect the house and the old barn.

The addition created interest all right—nearly started a scandal for old Cap Larsen, who lived there alone!

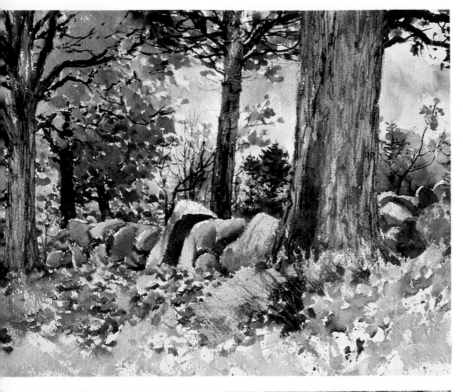

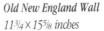

I almost overlooked one of these scenes because I was so busy painting the other. First I painted Old New England Wall. *The loosely penciled wall was washed in with a light gray, leaving edges and bits of white showing. Variation of value as well as color were added into the wet wash. Eventually the stronger areas were painted in with more definition in the foreground. Rugged maple trunks were washed in and brush-handled for character. Loose foliage and foreground were rendered next and the sky was painted in last, around trunks, limbs, and leaves.*

As I was packing up to leave, I saw the setting for Family Graveyard, *just off the road on a light rise. The setting was a beautiful and quiet story of the end of labor, showing respect for the past, tribute to our ancestors, and a reminder of at what cost we have land today. I unpacked and got back to work.*

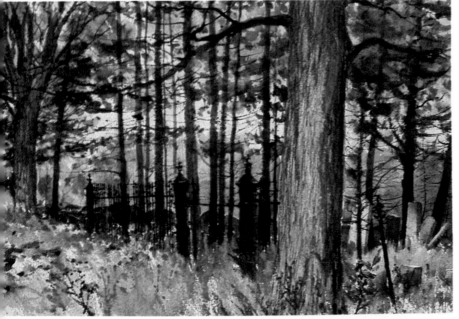

Family Graveyard
13³/₄ × 21³/₄ inches

some large ones, it was a story indeed. What sweat it must have taken to clear the fields of such a clutter! How could the early farmer ever have moved some of these blocks of granite? The painting finished, I packed up to leave, turned the car around and drove less than a hundred yards and there, unnoticed earlier, was an ancient family graveyard, so common to New England. Several enjoyable hours were spent doing the painting "Family Graveyard."

DECIDING WHAT TO INCLUDE

When you've chosen a subject and start planning a composition, it's necessary to stick to your first impression or intention and not allow yourself to be distracted. If other ideas intrude, make a note of them and perhaps set them aside for another painting at a later date. In the beginning this is hard to do. It is natural to include too much and add meaningless frills. Constantly remind yourself to restrict your efforts to the single most interesting thing you have in mind for your painting. One of the values of a sketch book is that all exploratory thumbnail sketches are there, available for future study. They often yield entirely new ideas, other than the ones originally pursued.

ous, old-fashioned, horse-operated sorghum press; I drove on a couple of miles, but finally decided to go back. There was an excellent place to park and several hours were spent doing a most unusual and interesting painting. We did not see another press the remainder of our trip. When you see a good subject and can stop safely, do so! Two more examples:

I was driving down a New Hampshire backroad on a sunny October day and was inspired to do the old stone wall in "Old New England Wall." With colorful maples lined up and an accumulation of smaller rocks together with

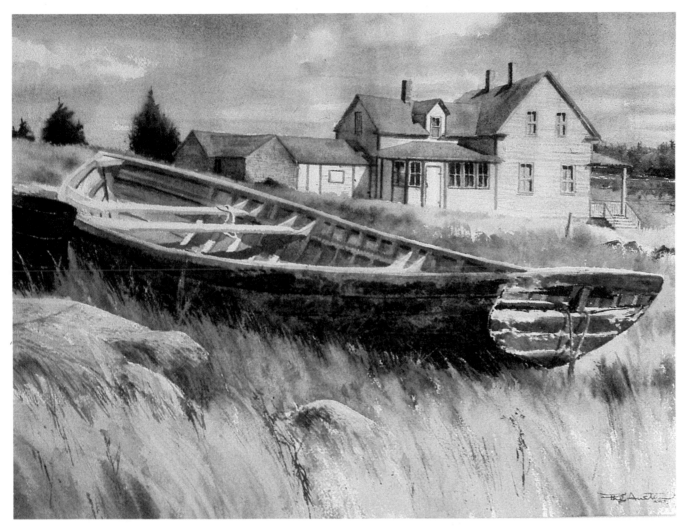

In a Nova Scotia Field
20½ × 28 inches

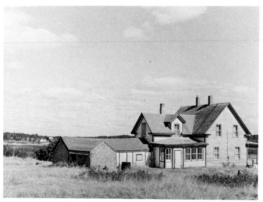

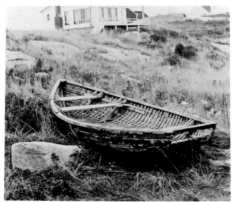

When you're deciding which parts of a scene to include and which to leave out, don't dismiss the possibility of adding new elements. The photograph of an interesting structure near Digby, Nova Scotia, didn't make a striking composition by itself. But when I added the battered old boat from Peggy's Cove—with its chipped paint, shadowed ribs, and sunlit seat boards—the composition worked.

The movement in this painting begins with the light in the foreground, travels to the light rocks, rusty dark drum, curving bow of the boat, evergreens on the horizon, far clouds, chimneys of the house, sunny end of the building, darker middle ground, and back into the end of the boat.

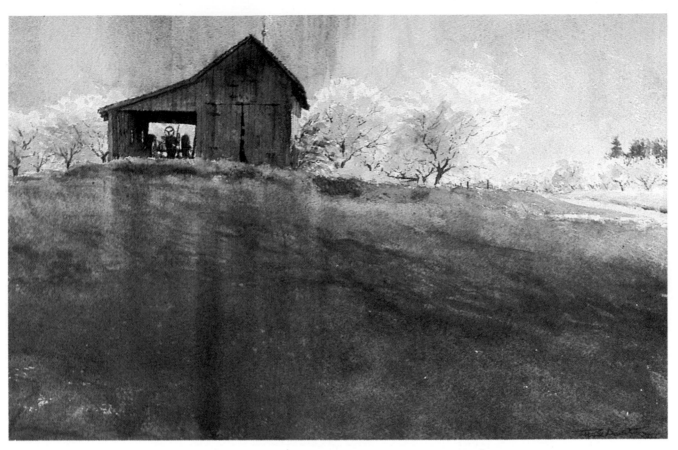

Cherry Orchards
14 × 21½ inches

The choice of a low viewpoint for this painting placed the center of interest high in the upper left corner, which is where most viewers look first, and created a large, simple foreground area. This accentuates the division between nature and man-made forms that first attracted me to the scene.

The orchard was in stark contrast to the weathered gray shed, with the tractor a beautiful little silhouette. Vertical brush strokes were put in to darken the sky against nearby trees and break up the foreground.

VIEWPOINT

Early in your planning a point of view must be established. Should you be looking up to the main object of interest, or down into it? Will you use a low horizon with very little foreground and a great deal of sky? Or would it be better to break objects out of the top of the painting and use a predominance of foreground? Your whole arrangement of the composition depends on your choice at this point. This is where several quick thumbnail sketches can be of great help.

CENTER OF INTEREST

Once you've decided what you want to paint and why, decide on a location for the center of interest. How much of the painting will it occupy? How can you emphasize it? Will you use value contrast, color contrast, or both? Will increased detail help?

A fairly safe rule is to avoid centering objects within the composition, though exceptions are sometimes valid. Placing objects off-center and varying the division of space help toward pleasing results. Also, the grouping of objects suggests their relationships.

For example, a tree closer to a house than to the margin of the painting would suggest shelter, shade, or concealment for the house. Two

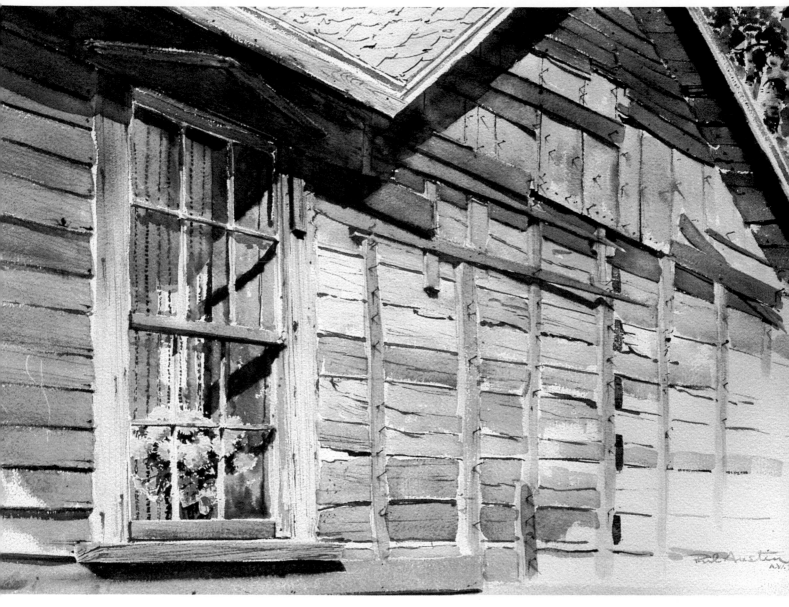

figures closer to each other than to other objects in the painting would suggest some kind of relationship between them.

Duplicating areas of equal size, interest, or color tends to create competition for interest. Several trees with the same trunk diameter, or placed the same distance apart, are likely to give a monotonous effect. Refraining from placing equally competing objects on both sides of a painting, choosing instead to make one smaller or more subdued in color, value, or contrast so that no comparison is invited, will also improve the composition. Varying the size, shape, and color of rocks in a wall will prevent the wall from looking like a row of bowling balls. Fence posts varying a bit in size, color, and position will be more interesting than a straight row, evenly spaced. Give constant thought to the avoidance of tedium.

If the center of interest is in the center or too close to any of the edges, you'll risk a static composition. Here, the window is about a third of the way from the left edge of the painting and the bright flowers in it are just a little less than a third of the way from the bottom edge—a pleasing placement.

This old log cabin exterior showed a varied history, battens, siding, window trim, desertion, and gradual deterioration of the original logs. An old lace curtain remained in the sole window on the east wall. I couldn't resist adding to the story by placing the pot of chrysanthemums in that east window. Now the old place was the humble residence of a cheerful soul, who loved beauty.

East Window
21 × 28 inches
Collection of Mrs. Phil Austin

19

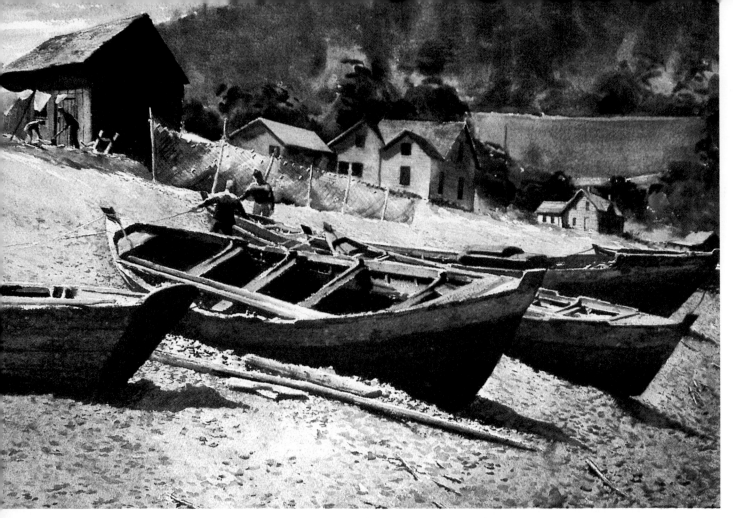

On the Beach,
Mont St. Pierre
21 × 28½ inches

The lines of this composition direct the eye through the painting. The viewer is first attracted to the boat in the foreground, and the light edges of the boat and its oars lead the eye up the beach to the clothes hanging on the line behind it. The eye then moves along the white shapes of the houses to the most distant boats, which lead back to the starting place.

The heavy boats in the foreground, suggesting rugged work, and the houses behind them say a lot about living and working in this community along the St. Lawrence.

DIRECTING THE EYE

Patterns of motion can be set up in a composition so that the subjects do not become static. There are a number of ways to do this. In a landscape, a road or a path may lead into the painting. This does not mean it should be an obvious shape—it can be a hint of a traveled area, with traces of wear, trampled grass, or bits of roadway showing between clumps of grass. Tell as much of a story as you possibly can in this sort of a situation. It is never wise to shut a viewer out of a painting by placing a barrier all the way across the foreground, such as a railroad track, a picket fence without a gate, or a stone wall without a gap. Even a place

where bushes or foliage can stop the horizontal motion momentarily will help.

Try to bridge a strong horizontal in the foreground with some object—even if it is only a strong shadow, as in "Farm on the Winter Hill." Use repetition of color in varying amounts and strengths in various parts of the painting to create a motion pattern. Varying light and dark areas will also help.

A tree, building, or other object near the edge of the painting can serve to carry attention vertically over the painting surface. A scrap or two of blue sky in a gray overcast may then pick up the motion from the tree or building and carry it across the top of the painting to another object such as a larger tree, a telephone pole, a silo, a windmill, or perhaps a chimney on a house. From there the motion might lead to a window reflecting the sky, then on down to a horizontal puddle with reflections in it. Plan this directional pattern very carefully so that the eye will follow it involuntarily, thus "reading" the painting and not stopping in confusion, straying out at a corner or somewhere along the side of the painting.

This directional flow needs a starting point. It could be a path into the painting somewhere in the foreground, or perhaps foam on a large wave; or light on a large rock, a clump of bright foliage, an open gate in a wall; an object like a wagon or a boat obviously moving into the painting. The possibilities are endless. Sometimes an object of particular interest can start that motion within the painting and the various ways mentioned may be used to keep it circling.

Areas of contrast will also draw attention to different parts of the painting—silhouetting dark objects against light or bright color against dull color. Action in the painting will also accomplish this.

OTHER COMPOSITION CONSIDERATIONS

Corners of a painting need special attention, lest they draw too much interest. You will do well to avoid the use of any strong line coming directly to a corner, which unavoidably draws attention to it. We can deepen color in a corner, reduce details, or in some instances use a light corner, which picks up the motion from other light areas in the painting. Sometimes a large simple object which breaks out of the picture can effectively close up a corner.

When an awkward dead space occurs between an object and an edge of the painting it's a good idea either to get rid of the space by moving the object into it, or to enlarge the space by moving the object away and thus toward the center of the picture. Should you make the former choice, the object can even be cropped by the picture's edge, but be sure that enough of it remains for it to be identified. In the case of the latter choice the formerly dead space will become a valid shape that takes its place in your composition.

Placing objects where edges just touch causes obvious contact points, while coinciding lines of different objects may create awkward areas, which attract unwanted attention.

A painting that is abstract in character can rely purely on shape for composition, whereas a representational painting relies on recognition of those shapes as well. For this reason if part of an object—a wagon wheel or a barrel, let's say—should extend outside an edge of the painting you must make sure that what remains is not only a pleasing shape which fits your composition, but also identifies itself as a wagon wheel or a barrel. When this is done successfully the viewer supplies the missing part of the object with his mind's eye.

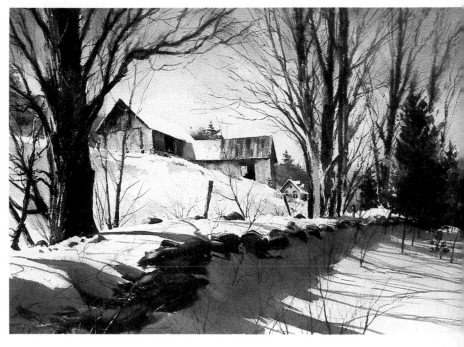

The beautiful snow-covered stone wall pulls the viewer into this picture. The strong values of rocks and shadow with adjacent trees hold the attention, while more distant buildings and wood create the atmosphere.

Farm on the Winter Hill
21 × 29 inches

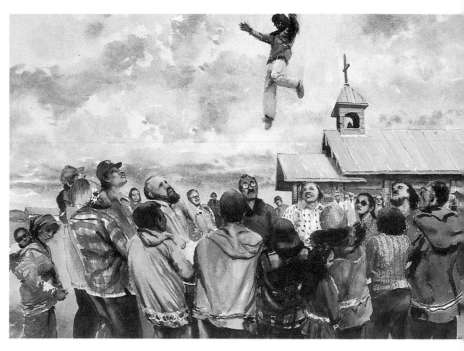

Blanket Toss, Kotzebue
21½ × 29½ inches
Collection of Mr. and Mrs. Leon Zygmun

In this painting everything is intended to emphasize the flying figure. The clouds form a triangle of tone and create an area of light behind the boy in the air. All figures pull away from the blanket in the center, all eyes are on the figure in the air. The upraised hand breaks the top margin to suggest height. The church is simple in detail, as are all the surroundings, so that the story is told simply and directly.

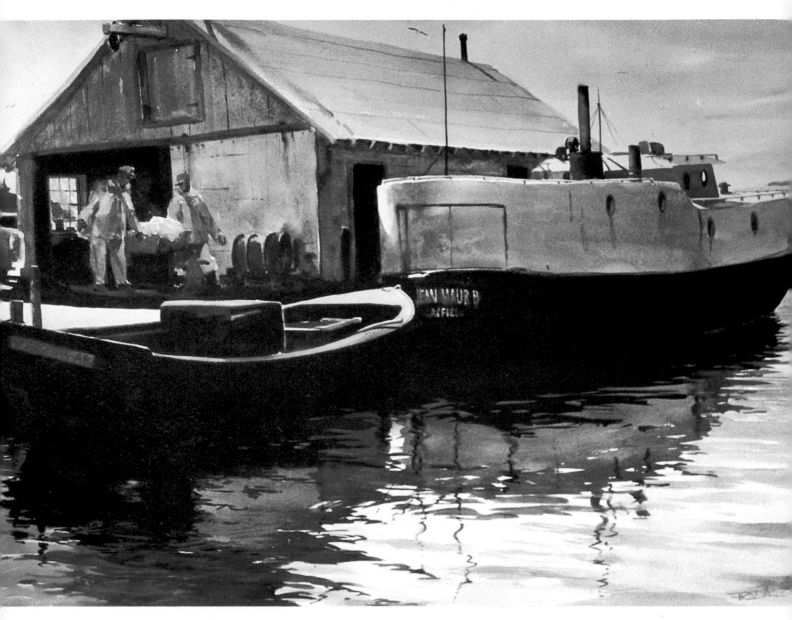

This painting has a strong pattern of lights and darks. The boat hulls blend with their reflections to create a strong dark shape, which contrasts with the white of the rear boat and the sunlit dock. The light values of the fish shed blend with similar areas, as do the docks. The figures of the fishermen blend at some points, contrast and stand out at others, contributing to a fluid painting.

Dock at Bayfield
21 × 29 inches

3. Developing a Pattern of Lights and Darks

THE IMPORTANCE OF VALUES

Values are a powerful design factor. If you fail to consider values as you paint, your work is likely to either be flat and drab, or contain competing areas of vibrating colors.

A pattern of lights and darks can help draw attention to the center of interest. A large simple area of extreme dark will really emphasize a small light area such as a window opening, and a large area of light such as a field of snow will highlight a dark little gesture of a man or animal. Middle values can dominate most of the composition, allowing smaller areas of very light or very dark values to become extremely important.

Value differences also add depth and dimension to the objects in your painting. Without value contrasts the forms in the picture will appear flat. For example, if you are painting a building in bright sunlight, regardless of what color it is, the side towards the sun should be considerably lighter than the side away from the light.

The more you plan and exploit the use of value contrasts, the stronger the feeling of form and depth on your two-dimensional painting surface and the greater the illusion of reality.

LEARNING TO CONTROL VALUES

Value is determined on a scale from black to white. It is the amount of light an object or color reflects, dark values being near the black end of the scale, light values obviously being nearer the white end, with intermediate values between. Middle values usually compose the major part of most paintings with the extremes of light and dark interacting with them.

All colors have a value—that is, a place where they fall on the black-and-white value scale. Squinting at the color so that value rather than color is seen will help to determine this. Colors by themselves, without regard for value, seldom produce a good painting. The painting must be held together by a pattern of light and dark. Otherwise the result may be a "patchwork quilt" that will lack any unity or mood.

Thus if you wish to use a color like yellow or orange, for example, and it does not have a dark enough value for a particular area of your painting, you must modify that color to give it the value you wish it to have (see pages 45-46).

You should plan the entire value pattern for your painting at the outset, so that your color conforms to your value plan. This is where vermilion and ultramarine become important. You can mix any value on the black-and-white scale with them. This wash of gray, beginning just below white and graduating all the way to an approximation of black, shows how darks created with vermilion and ultramarine have more "life" than similar values created with black pigment. (If you have trouble with these values looking slightly purple, add a minute amount of orange.) Since it is much easier to recognize value on the black-and-white scale than it is in the colors, you can mix any value below the middle of the scale and add color without changing the value. It is difficult to find colors which have dark value, other than earth colors such as burnt umber, but it is easy to mix as dark a value as you wish and then convert it to a red, a red-brown, a yellow-brown, a dark green, a dark blue, or a purple, as needed.

Small additions of vermilion, orange, or green will take the dark in any color direction you wish, with little or no change in value, whereas the use of a strong earth color for darks will not allow a color added to it to influence the dark very much.

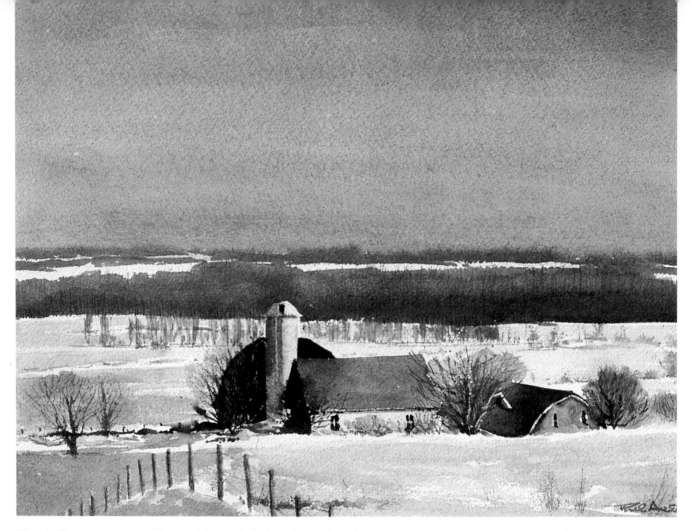

Winter Valley
11³/₄ × 15⁵/₈ inches

The middle and dark values of the house and farm buildings contrast with the light value of the snowy field, calling attention to the center of interest immediately. The dark shape of distant trees also forms a nice counterpoint to the large area of middle value in the sky.

For colors above a middle value, the smallest amount of vermilion, ultramarine, or both will darken the value. The darker grays can easily be modified also with very small amounts of color, while still maintaining their value; a speck of orange added will make a warmer gray, a bit of cerulean will make it cooler and bluer, a bit of yellow will produce a greenish gray, and so on. We are really painting value and making our colors conform to our value plan.

Cadmium orange is a potent color and must be used *sparingly*. A little goes a long way. Should your mixed dark for some reason appear slightly purple when you wish it to be neutral, a small touch of orange will immediately remedy this. The same is true of the grays. Orange, you will soon discover, is a good short cut where normally you might add both red and yellow. Following this method allows you to make subtle changes in color and/or

All colors have both hue and value. The top band here shows a range of values from just below white to almost black. The bottom band shows that same value range in color.

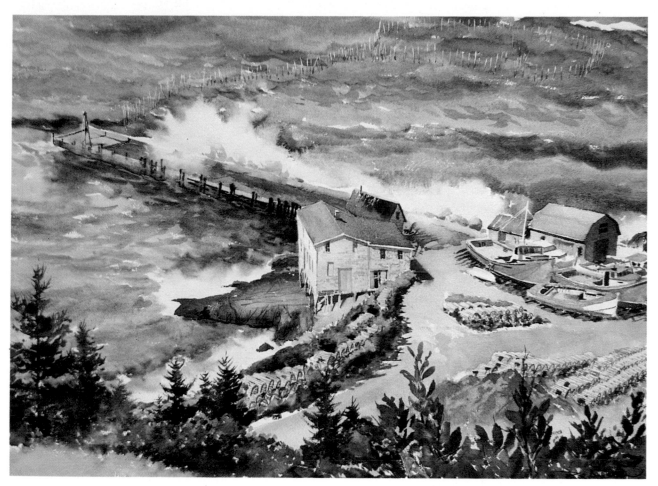

values as you move about the painting.

Working with small sketches, either pencil thumbnails or watercolors, gives the opportunity to experiment with value ideas until you find the most effective way to use them in any particular subject you are planning to paint.

If you find that you are experiencing difficulty determining the value of a particular color when painting on location, try using an inexpensive "instant" camera with black-and-white film. The resulting print will tell you at a glance what value to give that particular area. You may decide to change the color somewhat and increase or reduce its value as well. You may find it helpful at times to photograph your finished painting in black and white so that you can more readily analyze your values.

One important thing to remember is that you are not a camera, accepting colors and values as they are, but are free to manipulate and adjust value and color to your advantage.

When painting this exciting area along the Bay of Fundy, I never did develop a good value pattern. The color is good, but this painting needs considerable study with sketches and readjustment of values. Stronger contrasts in the village would improve it, keeping the viewer's eye from traveling down the dock and out of the painting.

High Tide at Sandy Cove
21¹/₂ × 29 inches

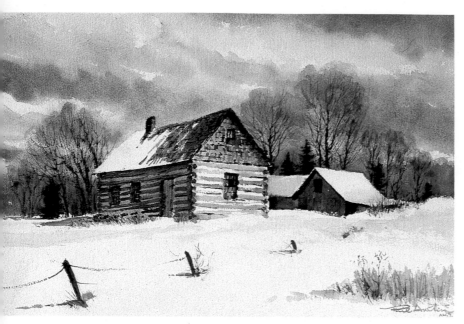

This painting, done as a classroom demonstration, shows the use of dark against light—note the cabin roof, light on the left and dark on the right. The patches of light and dark on the light end of the cabin create a harlequin effect.

Details were minimized in the sheds behind, while trees on the left of the cabin blended with the cabin for a lost edge. The light end of the cabin is also nearly a lost edge with the snow, in contrast with the stark division between snow and the rear shed. The sky is low hanging, snow clouds suggest a cold temperature. The foreground has little change in value and limited detail so that it does not compete with the cabin details.

Left in the Cold
14 × 21¹⁄₂ inches

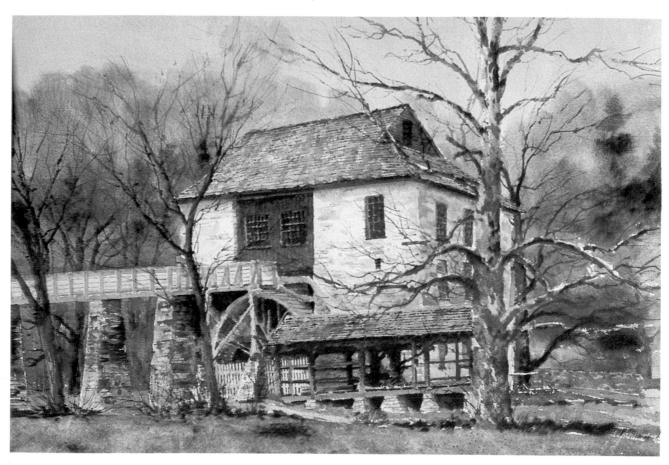

This painting of a marvelous old stone mill that's been reconstructed in an Indiana state park shows how a deep cloud shadow, dark sky, or group of trees behind a building will highlight it. The mill's sluice with its stone pylons, the sawing platform in the foreground, and the filigree of tattered sycamores provide a beautiful contrast to the simple block of the mill.

November at Spring Mill
21 × 29 inches

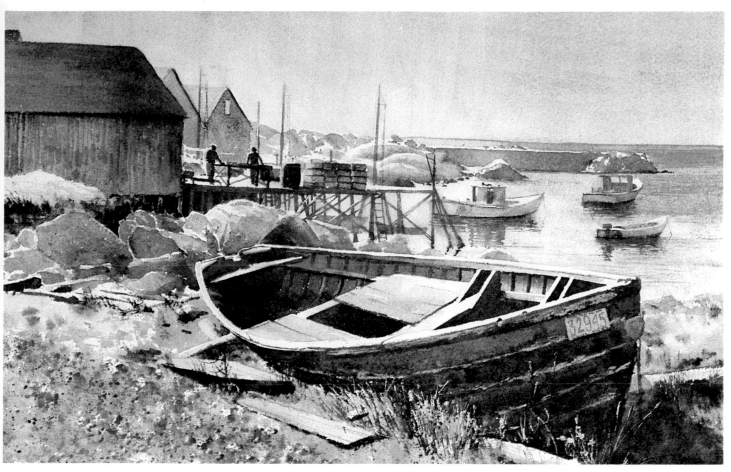

Afternoon Light at Indian Harbor

14 × 21½ inches

This painting is predominantly composed of values of gray, so it was important to hold delicate areas of light, such as the grass against the boat hull, light surfaces on rocks, figures etched in light, and chips in the paint. Since many of these small light accents are in wash areas, it was convenient to use liquid mask before flowing on large areas of wash. Subtle color added to these washes help liven up the gray values.

USING VALUE TO CREATE INTEREST

"Afternoon Light at Indian Harbor," a Nova Scotia painting, demonstrates clearly the principle of changing value in various areas to build contrast and center of interest. The light-splashed areas on parts of the boat in the foreground, such as the seats and brackets and the gunwales, are extremely light while shadows are extremely dark, especially under the rear seat (lightening upward along the rib structure), and in the center area between seats, as well as the near side of the boat beneath the gunwale and bow.

Notice the changing value in the large rocks behind this boat. The nearest fish shed darkens toward the right as it approaches the lighter area where the men are working. The light floods on the dock around them. Their silhouettes, as well as the table, barrel, and dock, seem to increase the intensity of this flood of light, by contrast.

Even the distant sheds darken upward to emphasize the light area below them. The distant rocks are very light, but the distant seawall darkens gradually toward the right, away from the area of extreme light. Decks of anchored lobster boats pick up bits of pure light as well, to contrast with deeper shadow areas of interiors and water lines.

The water itself is almost without color or value near the dock, but deepens gradually toward the right. The lower left front corner of the painting has dark gravel tones in contrast with lighter grass beyond it. Even the sky lightens in value to the left and right of the center of interest. All of the above-mentioned touches bring interest into the area where we wish to center it. This should be done in such a way that it is effective without being obvious.

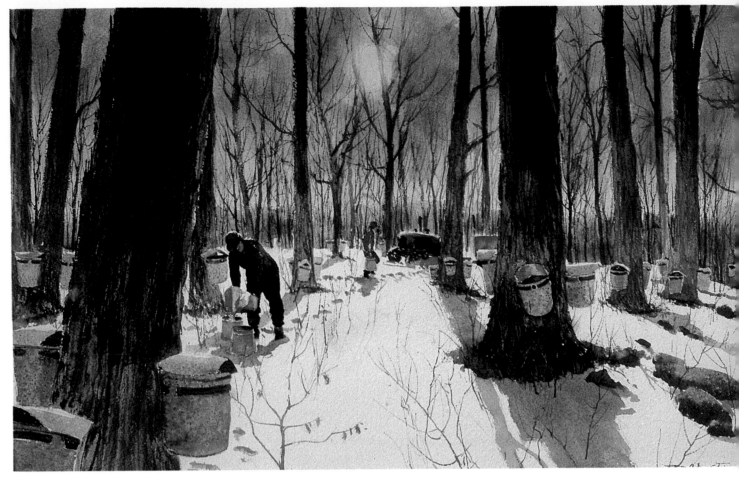

Back lighting forms strong shadows in this painting, creating an interesting composition. The brush handle is a real aid in doing maple tree bark, and salt in the wet wash on the sap buckets really mottles it like galvanized metal.

Having helped the neighbors a bit in their sugar bush as a kid, I take real pleasure in doing frequent paintings of this old and interesting operation.

Morning in the Sugar Bush
14 × 21½ inches

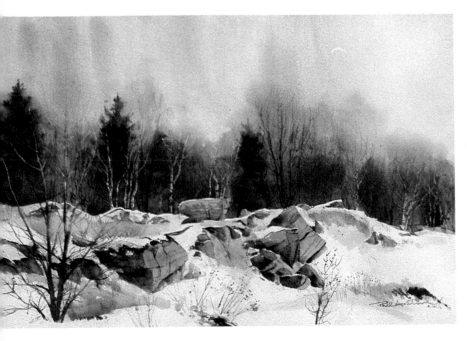

I started out in sunshine to paint this location, but clouds moved in, to my disappointment. However, the soft light brought out the warm grays of limestone, the background of woods, and the soft blue-gray snow shadows. The evergreens blended into the surrounding trees. The sky wash required a bit of cadmium yellow pale for the haze. A few days later I went over again to paint in sunshine. The shadows were deep and harsh—the mystery of the place had vanished.

Winter Limestone Quarry
14 × 21½ inches

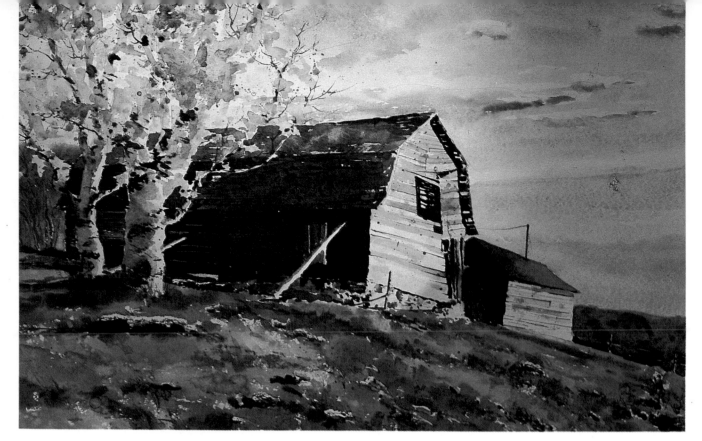

Evening Light, Lost Lake Road

21½ × 29 inches

Side lighting creates the mood of early evening in this painting. The simplified lights and darks dramatize the old buildings and the sturdy birches beside them. Note the buildup of light against dark at the building corners.

DIRECTION OF LIGHT

When you're developing a value pattern, you must also determine the direction from which light is falling on your subject. Should you look for back lighting, flat lighting, side lighting, or shadowless lighting? This is an important choice.

A subject which does not draw a second glance will, at another time, in a different light, become an exciting scene to paint. Painting on location offers you the opportunity to observe the importance of the lighting. If you have the time, an excellent idea is to check out painting areas at different times of day under different weather and light conditions. Thus you can develop the habit of reviewing lighting possibilities, so that when you plan a value pattern you can make the best choice.

You might even get a detailed map of your particular painting area, mark favorite spots, make notes as to when lighting is best, what season is best, what weather conditions are most exciting. Then plan your painting trips to take advantage of these facts.

An example of this is the painting "Winter Limestone Quarry." Planning to do it on a sunny, snowy day, I drove twenty miles, only to have dark clouds move in. However, the subdued light had given it soft color, subtle values, an air of mystery, and a mood which was far more exciting to paint than the harsh light and strong shadows of a sunny day.

Generally the greatest extremes of value occur in backlighting situations. This can produce dramatic effects. Under the usually prevalent conditions of side lighting, the forms can be delineated in many interesting ways. Diagonal shadows can show changes of plane and establish exciting compositional shapes. Strong contrasts between the light and dark sides of buildings create the feeling of solid forms. Reflected lights can be used to lighten areas and create interest in the shadows.

Variety in value will be present also in flat lighting of subjects, but in a lesser degree. Contrast in value is effective in separating the principal subject material from its surroundings. A deep cloud shadow or a dark sky behind an object such as a building will highlight it even though the painting has flat lighting.

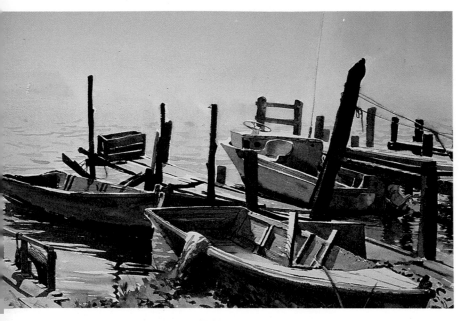

Morning Glare, Port Salerno
14 × 21 inches
Collection of Mr. and Mrs.
Gerald Slade

BACK LIGHTING

Back lighting produces dark objects against light surroundings. In "Morning Glare, Port Salerno," boat piers and pilings form an interesting dark pattern against almost pure light used as negative space, as you can see clearly in the thumbnail sketch of the painting. The next thumbnail again uses a boat, piers, pilings, and fishing equipment, as well as a distant headland of lighter value, backlighted by a bit of evening sky, and its reflection. The third backlighting sketch, a boy sitting on a beached boat, also shows an interesting silhouette against lighter distance and surf.

Dramatic back lighting creates the effect of morning light, above and far left, and softer back light using sky reflections gives the feeling of evening, center. A lad sitting indolently watching the Baja surf, near left, is the perfect subject for back lighting.

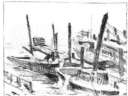
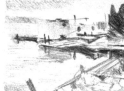
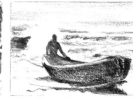

FLAT LIGHTING

Flat lighting often results in light objects against a darker background, as shown in the first thumbnail sketch. In "Afternoon in Sitka" and its sketch, the main street of Sitka, Alaska, is shown with its buildings flooded with afternoon light against a dark mountain. The third thumbnail shows farm buildings and foreground picking up light with darker trees flanking them.

Flat lighting, which often results in light objects against a dark background, was used for the snow-covered rock escarpment, far left below; Sitka, Alaska, at left and in the center sketch below; and farm scene, near left below.

Afternoon in Sitka
14 × 21½ inches

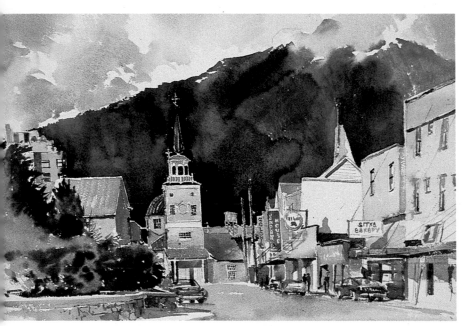

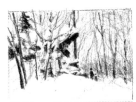
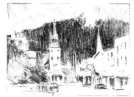
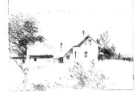

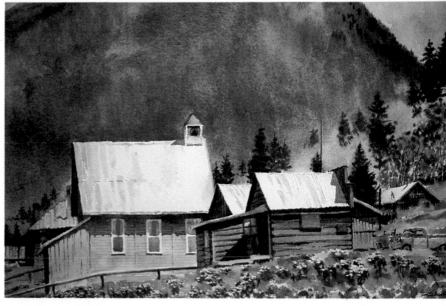

*Hahn's Peak Village,
Colorado
21½ × 28½ inches*

SIDE LIGHTING

The Colorado mining town in "Hahn's Peak
Village, Colorado" shows the effect of strong
diagonals from side lighting, combined with
some top lighting. Because of the inclined surfaces, the roofs catch strong light. This type of
light generally provides strong patterns.

The second thumbnail of side lighting
shows the use of strong shadows created by
the low side lighting of winter months. The
farm scene shows side lighting picking up scattered lights and creating darks as well.

*Side lighting creates horizontal shadows
and strong value patterns. I used it for the
mining town, near right and above; winter
scene, center; and farm in winter, far right.*

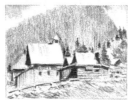 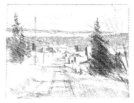 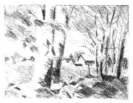

SHADOWLESS LIGHT

Shadowless light creates much more subtle
compositions with fewer strong contrasts than
side lighting. Moody paintings are very likely
to require shadowless light. The barn and winter orchard in "January Sky" provide opportunity to use large simple areas of value. The
sketch of a late fall scene depends on values of
objects to create the pattern, as does the sketch
for a painting of a tide marsh.

*Shadowless light is good for moody settings
such as the winter orchard, left and below
at near right; fall scene, center; and tide
marsh, far right below.*

*January Sky
11½ × 15⅝ inches*

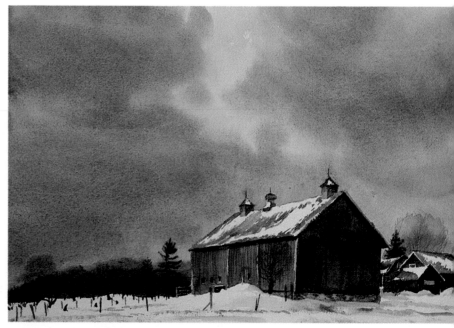

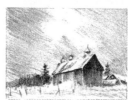 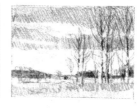 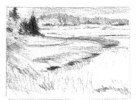

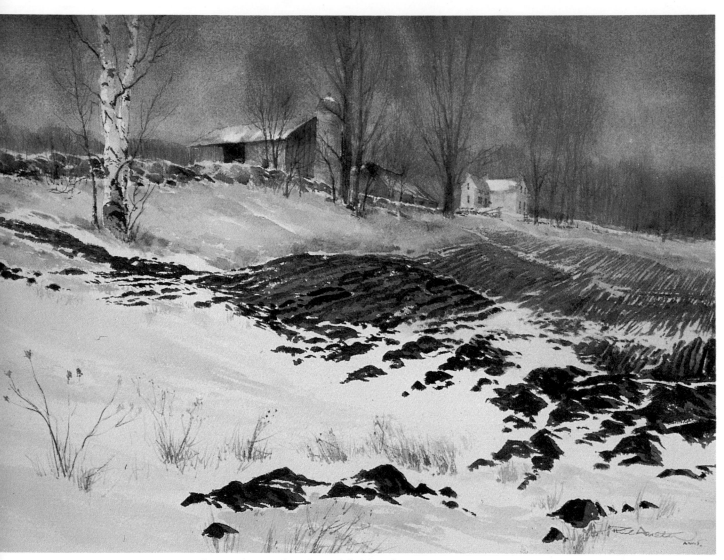

Fog on Kari's Ridge
21 × 29 inches

This painting of a plowed field with new snow drifted in the furrows uses contrasting values and textures, but the overall effect is one of harmony. The deeper snow in the front left made excellent negative space and snow on the house roof was a small repeat. The fog was introduced to push the farm back into the distance slightly.

4. Creating Contrast and Harmony

In the process of making a painting interesting and expressive, it is important that the final result is a well-thought-out blend of all the parts. To make an effective blend, you need to use both harmony and contrast. An active center of interest might be offset by a large simple space, for example, a different use of contrast than that of value. Strong bright color might be complemented by areas of more neutral color.

Even though contrasts such as these add interest to a painting, a sense of harmony is also important. Positive and negative spaces must work well together, for example, or you can create a unified pattern of shapes by using overlapping.

POSITIVE AND NEGATIVE SPACE

Negative space is frequently thought of as the unpainted area of a painting, forming a loose vignette around certain parts of the painting (as in "Spring Trillium"). This way of handling composition is but a part of what negative space can do for a painting. Since it is inactive space, it must be kept simple, containing no strong contrasts or elaborate detail. It must be planned together with the positive space which constitutes the objects of greatest interest. Positive space is "where the action is."

Negative space can be very useful in creating mood. A winter landscape, for instance, might have an extremely large foreground of snow with little or no detail (such as saplings, weeds, or twigs), suggesting utter silence.

Negative space can also be used to create the opposite mood. A large area of tumbling clouds mixed with smaller patches of blue sky, a good deal of texture, changing values, and a lot of action—and an area that could have been simple negative space suddenly becomes the center of interest. The balance of the painting could then be a low horizon with simple shapes and small areas of contrasting color and value and a foreground of quiet color with very little or no detail—negative space. The negative space in a painting is a quiet area contrasting with the very active and exciting part of the painting. This type of contrast of areas is important.

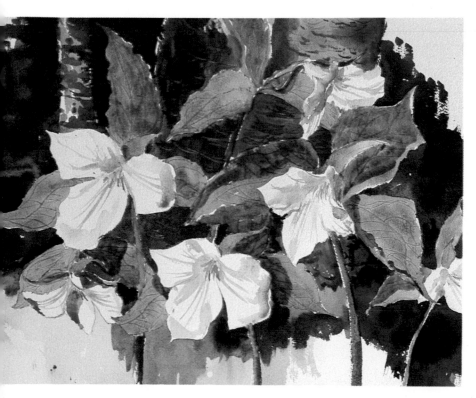

The white vignetted corners of this painting keep the white flowers from floating in a sea of dark value. The leaves provide an intermediate step between areas of extreme dark and light. A faint wash in some of the vignetted area sets it apart from the pure white of the flowers.

Spring Trillium
11³/4 × 15⁵/8 inches

33

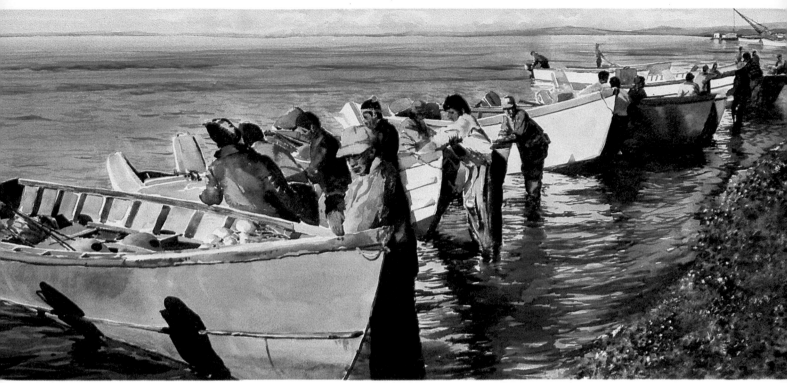

Waiting to Unload,
Kotzebue

15 × 40 inches
Collection of Mr. and Mrs.
Delbert Hargrave

The overlapping of the boats helps tie this busy scene together, creating harmony. Darks are very carefully accented against light areas, and the simple boat shapes contrast with the more complex human forms and with the shimmering reflections. An ambitious use of figures, this was painted from slides taken on an August evening above the Arctic Circle.

OVERLAPPING

Harmony of composition is maintained by interlocking areas of interest into a logical pattern rather than leaving objects scattered all over the painting. By overlapping shapes it is possible to avoid this kind of discord. Explore all possibilities in the thumbnail planning stage, even to the extent of considering whether the clouds will be overlapped by trees, buildings, or mountains. Plan the overlap of open areas to create a more interesting use of negative space as well.

This principle is found in "Cold Moving In, Jackson Harbor." Dry marsh grass in the immediate foreground overlaps the negative space of water and the rowboat. The front boat overlaps the dock. The dock is overlapped by the fishing boat tied at the end of it. This fishing boat, a "gillnetter," overlaps a distant one. Old pilings and a light pole on the dock overlap more distant water (containing reflections), the farther shore of the inlet, and a log dock and fish sheds. The two gillnetters tied up to the distant dock overlap that dock, a fish shed, the distant shore, and a bit of sky. You will find it a simple matter in the early planning stage to move things around to interlock in this manner. Do this in the beginning, lest you end up with objects in an awkward place resulting in very poor composition.

A further function of overlapping is to give the illusion of depth, causing objects to appear to recede from the eye of the viewer. By placing a tree partially in front of or behind a building or another object, or by carrying a fore-

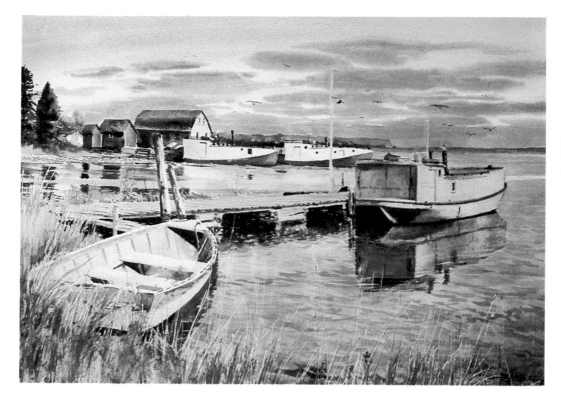

Cold Moving In, Jackson Harbor
21 × 29 inches

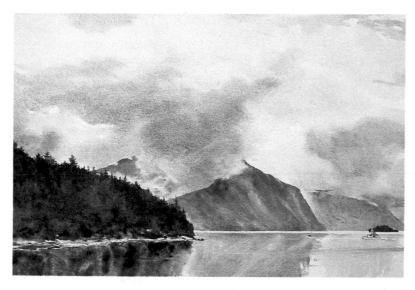

A series of overlapping shapes unifies this painting, from the grass that overlaps the boat in the foreground to the two gillnetters that overlap the distant dock.

The cloud-draped mountains along the Inside Passage of Alaska provide an excellent example of the depth that can be created by overlap. The calm water and reflections double the effect. This painting is composed almost entirely of varying washes of gray blue, the green nearby point and the green islands being the only exceptions.

Calm Passage
21 1/2 × 29 inches
Collection of Mr. and Mrs. Patrick Riley

ground shadow across an empty area and up the side of a building, tree, or slope, we can overlap to strengthen the composition.

Depth in a painting is further emphasized by reducing the size of more distant objects, by reducing the intensity and value contrast of color, and by eliminating distant detail. In addition, a slight reduction of value at the points of overlap (see "Calm Passage") creates a feeling of atmosphere (space between overlapped objects).

Overlapping can delineate terrain in a landscape, as well as contour of an object. A shadow falling across an object will show clearly the ins and outs of the surface—like a log wall for instance, or a rugged rock.

For example, a landscape might have an interesting closeup of grass and weeds with wild flowers along the shoulder of a road entering the painting. A large tree in the near foreground could have a shadow following the contour of the roadside and continuing up over and across the road. This would show very clearly the dips and curves of the road.

A series of overlaps is very effective. A large foreground tree could overlap a tree in the middle distance, which would be less intense in color and value. A far simple hedgerow could lap distant farm buildings which in turn could lap more distant trees of bluer hue than the foreground color. These in turn could lap more neutral green hills and fields. The build-

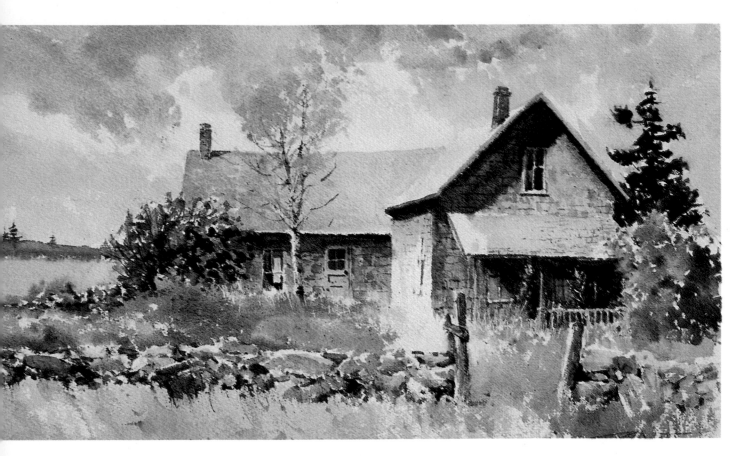

Norma Jean's Farm House
14 × 21½ inches
Collection of Mr. and Mrs.
Vincent Shiel

Lost edges like the ones in this painting contribute a sense of fluid motion. Note how the lower edge of the house is lost against the brightly lit grass and how similar values where the two roofs meet make those edges indistinct.

ings, further trees, and distant hills would have a minimum of simple detail.

A road going over a series of rises and hollows is another way overlapping could be used to delineate topography. The road would narrow each time it reappeared, and be overlapped by the wider portion of the road in the foreground.

LOST AND FOUND EDGES

Light is the most important factor with which an artist deals. God has given us a beautiful world, but without the gift of light, we could never be aware of that beauty! Where there's no light there's neither color nor variation in value.

An aspect of light and what it does that is important for successful painting is its effect on edges. Light, or absence of light, as the case may be, creates lost and found edges. Recognizing and using these in your painting will give your works a fluid quality.

Taking into consideration the direction from which light falls, you will see that all surfaces receiving it are light and those not directly receiving it are to varying degrees darker. In a painting as in nature, the edges between adjacent or overlapping light-struck surfaces are often lost due to the overall uniformity of value. The same holds for the darker surfaces that are close in value. This is often true regardless of local color.

Lost edges can help tie a composition together by unifying areas, making a single large shape out of several smaller ones. This is a phenomenon you can observe in nature by squinting your eyes as you look at a group of objects in a landscape or still life.

Every time you eliminate an edge where areas of similar value are adjacent you take another step toward tying the composition together with a fluid passage. It's natural to try to avoid allowing colors to run together. Yet when you study nature, you see all kinds of surfaces and objects that blend together. In fact, when you strain your eyes to separate these areas, you often cannot do so. You can employ these lost edges to create interest, mystery, and flow. Just as you enjoy reading a story where the writer does not bore you with every minute detail, but allows you to use your imagination to fill out the story, so you want to allow the viewers of your paintings to create their own stories.

As you need lost edges, so you also need sharply defined or found edges. These occur where very different hues or widely separated values meet. They cause a pleasing contrast to the lost edges and give the painting necessary definition. Watercolor painting offers every opportunity, because of the nature of the medium, to be fluid. If you fail to make the painting flow from one area to another because all its parts are too sharp and distinct, you'll have missed the whole reason for doing the painting in watercolor. Many failures are due to a lack of knowledge of lost and found edges.

INCREASING CONTRAST

Aldro Hibbard, an outstanding New England landscape painter, once suggested to me that "a surface is never the same from side to side or from top to bottom." He reasoned that any object or surface is always subject to varying influences such as sky light, reflected light, change due to contrast with some other hue or value, or change in value due to its shape. He further stated that if each surface was a continuous uniform hue or value, all the excitement that exists in nature would be lost. Learning to incorporate this into your painting habits will improve your work immeasurably. It will lead you to increase contrast at times, change color within an area with or without a change in value, observe and record reflected light or color, and become more aware of the influence of light.

"Norma Jean's Farm House" demonstrates both lost and found edges and changing values. The tawny grass in the foreground changes somewhat in color, and even more in value. It is light against the dark pockets of shadow in the rock wall, darker against the light flooding the top of this wall, equal value in some places with the rocks, and lighter, forming a lost edge where it meets the light on the left-hand side of the building.

The slanting porch roof lightens toward the left as it meets the darker shingles of the front wall. The roof on the wing of the house gradually becomes deeper in value toward the left as it meets the cloudy sky, but goes lighter as it meets the other roof, creating a lost edge.

The shingled walls of both the wing and the left side of the main structure deepen in value gradually as they approach the shadow below the eaves, forming a very strong found edge at the eave line. The bushes at the left of the house darken against this wall creating a lost edge, but the bushes on the right create a found edge against the dark green of the pine behind them.

The fence posts at the opening in the wall deepen as they go upward to create a found edge at their tops. The light on the left side of the two left posts creates a lost edge against the light grass, but another found edge against the darker shingles of the house. The clouds in the sky change value, going pure white against the roof on the farmhouse wing, but light gray to be lost against the other roof. You can examine this even further in the painting for yourself.

The treatment of edges can be used to great advantage in establishing centers of interest, in making little sparks of contrast, in creating excitement and a flow of light and dark values throughout the painting.

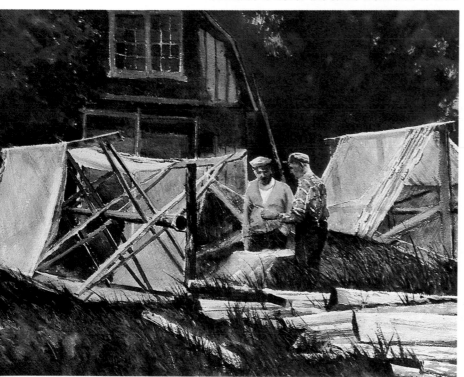

This painting uses contrast in several different ways. Dry brush grass contrasts with the large, simple net areas in both value and texture. The large, simple shapes of the trees and building also contrast with the detailed images of the fishermen and their racks.

Mending Nets
21½ × 29 inches

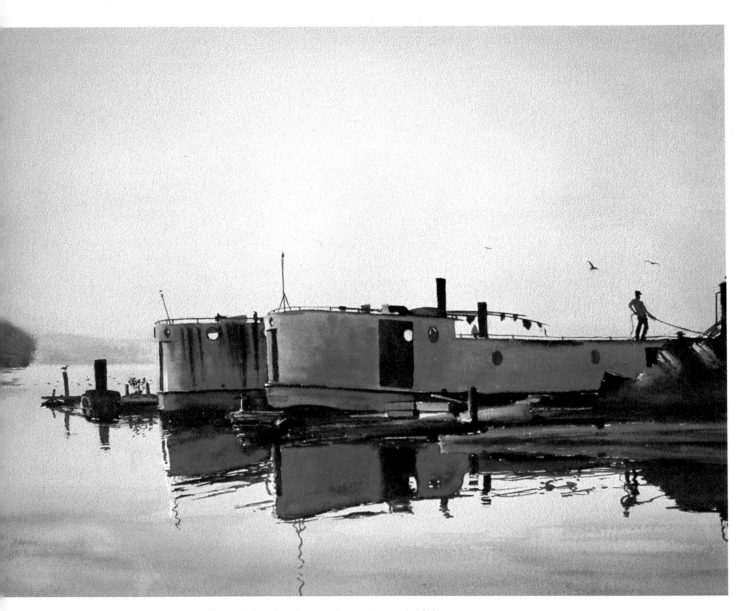

Day's End, Gills Rock
21 × 29 inches

The subdued color and pastel tones of the sky and water combine with the horizontal motion to create a mood of peace and rest.

5. Putting It All Together

CONVEYING EMOTION

When you look at a painting, does it arouse emotion, pleasure, nostalgia, fear, excitement, happiness, melancholy, peace, turmoil, or does it leave you completely apathetic? When someone views your work will it arouse an emotion or will it leave him or her indifferent? If emotional reaction to a subject prompts you to paint and you convey that emotion in all honesty, your painting becomes "you." You are then sharing yourself with others. Watercolor is an exceptionally good medium to convey emotion and mood, particularly if it is used in a fluid and spontaneous manner.

There are a number of things which will help to express feeling. Choice of color or combination of colors is important. Direction of stroke, softness or hardness of edges, values, amount of contrast—each plays a role in expressing an emotion. An excellent way to learn is by trying to express abstract ideas with a brush without any indication of a recognizable object. I have spent a two-hour period teaching this type of exercise in my workshop classes. I use a list—usually of opposites—such as hard, soft, sweet, sour, quiet, noisy, happy, sad, cold, hot, powerful, weak, rough,

smooth, disturbing, peaceful, and so on. They are done one at a time, confining each effort to a four-inch square. The students have five minutes in which to think and do it. It seems difficult at first, but with a little practice the ideas begin to flow. It's particularly helpful for several people to do this at the same time, comparing frequently to see how else it has been done.

Actually, expressing emotion is as important as the subject matter you choose. The more success you have in communicating emotions through your painting, the more satisfying the experience will become, and the more others will be able to relate to your work.

Power, for an example, is expressed in the sharp and rugged angles of the Rockies, as opposed to the old and worn mountains in other places. The horizontal landscapes and clouds of evening suggest peace and quiet. Even the gradually changing warm colors of evening sometimes add to the quietness. The soft grayness of fog may create a sense of silence, or aloneness and melancholy. Curving strokes of blowing grass may suggest gentleness whereas angled strokes indicate the power of wind, with tumbling clouds to match. This is but a brief suggestion of possibilities. Our world is full of symbols which we may find useful in expressing ourselves. All we have to do is look and think!

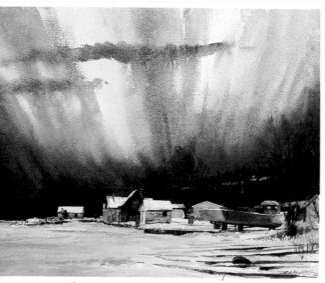

The unnatural light on the frozen harbor and snowy roofs combines with the explosive motion of light in the sky to create excitement and mystery, a very different mood from that in Day's End, Gills Rock.

Northern Lights at Gills Rock
21 × 29 inches

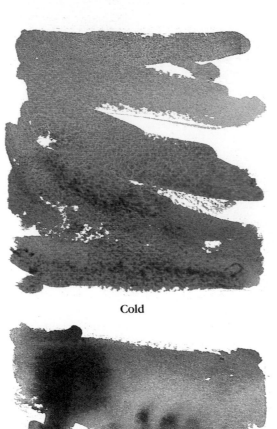

Cold

Hot

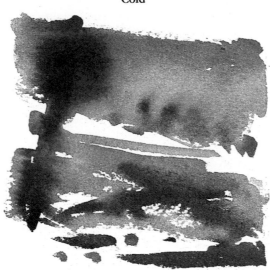

Melancholy

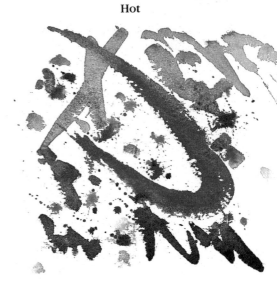

Gaiety

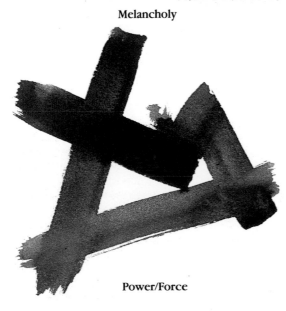

Power/Force

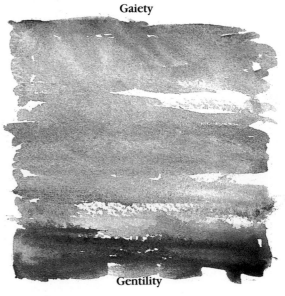

Gentility

The choice of color, direction of brush stroke, type of edges, values, and contrast all help convey emotion. These abstract paintings show just a few of the many moods a painter can convey by manipulating those elements.

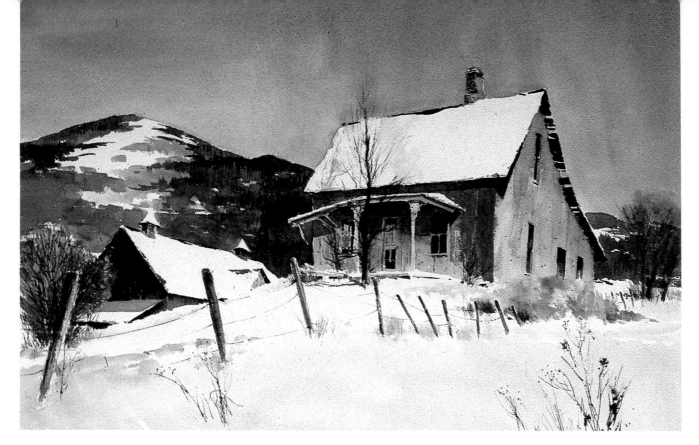

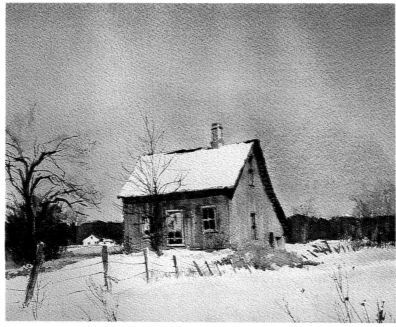

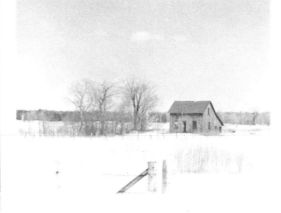

Neglected Dream
21 × 29 inches

Wisconsin Saltbox
11³/₄ × 15⁵/₈ inches

These two paintings show how experimenting with different compositions and value patterns is important to putting together a successful painting. Using the photograph of a New England "salt box"—in Wisconsin!—I first did the painting Wisconsin Saltbox. *I put snow on the roof and added a distant farm house to*

make a rather cheerful picture.

But after studying the painting, I decided much more could be said and did a number of exploratory thumbnails. I returned it to a New England setting and added the porch, barn, and mountain. In Neglected Dream, *note the concentration of pure white on roofs, open fields, and on the mountain, while there is a pale wash on the foreground areas. The red barn and yellow grass clumps serve as a relief to the cool grays. A light value on one fence post stands out against the dark bushes, while another darker post silhouettes against a white roof.*

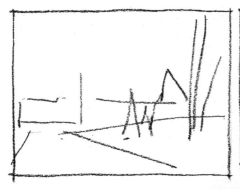
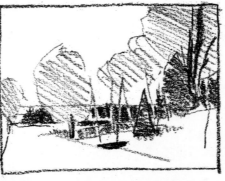
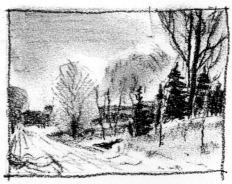

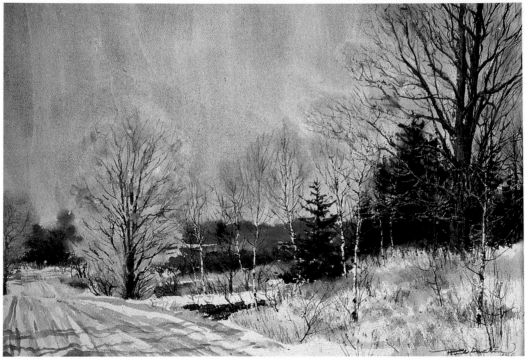

Afternoon Shadows,
Timberline Road
21 × 29 inches

The three thumbnail sketches for Afternoon Shadows, Timberline Road *indicate the process of planning a painting. First, analyze the subject for shapes, top left. Use triangles, rectangles, and circles to indicate the major shapes. Next, give a rough indication of the value of each shape, as shown at top center. Then complete the drawing with more detail, top right, so that it's ready to be developed into a painting.*

USING THUMBNAIL SKETCHES

As you're thinking about how to use composition, value and lighting, and contrast and harmony to create mood in your painting, write your ideas down so that you have a clear purpose before you start painting. Then begin to make thumbnail sketches with a soft pencil on the smooth paper of the sketch book. Because the paper is smooth and the lead is soft you can easily experiment, darkening values, lifting

others with a kneaded eraser, and moving objects until you are satisfied.

Decide at this point how much you want to include, what you will leave out, whether the format of your painting will be a conventional rectangle, a vertical, or a horizontal, or if a square or a circle would be better. Because these sketches are small, usually no more than 3″ × 4″, you need not get involved in a lot of drawing. You will be working mainly with ideas, smudging here, softening there, sometimes moving the margins of the sketch, studying values and use of space.

Try different arrangements, doing several trial sketches until you are satisfied you have worked out the best composition possible, one that will emphasize the main theme of your painting in the simplest and most direct manner.

In doing this planning you will have also imbedded in your mind a sort of mental blueprint of what you intend to do. You should also be considering what procedure you will need to follow, what areas to paint first, and whether to paint light or dark. You will have to time your return to some areas so that some edges

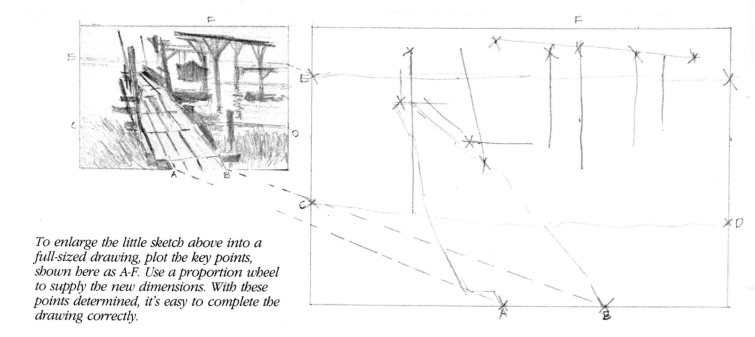

To enlarge the little sketch above into a full-sized drawing, plot the key points, shown here as A–F. Use a proportion wheel to supply the new dimensions. With these points determined, it's easy to complete the drawing correctly.

will run slightly together while others will remain separate.

You might make some notes to remind yourself of procedure. You will also have to decide how you will handle the subject: wet-on-wet, limited wet areas, dry brush, a wet approach on dry paper with a loaded brush, or a combination of these. Also you will need to decide what type of paper will work the best—rough, cold-press, or smooth? A given texture may lend itself particularly well to one type of subject, but not to another.

FINAL DRAWING

It is important to make your thumbnail sketches conform in scale and format to the intended painting. Once the final thumbnail sketch is chosen, there is a simple way to translate it to the sheet on which you intend to paint. Since it is often difficult to begin to draw objects in correct size and location on the large sheet, you should avoid a trial-and-error procedure. You can use an artist's proportion scale, available at art stores. This consists of two calibrated discs riveted together at the center so that they can revolve. If your sketch is 3 inches long and your painting is to be 29 inches long, set the discs at 3 and 29. Then any other comparisons made will be in proportion. For instance, a measurement of 1 inch will be 9¾ inches on the large sheet.

Plot a half dozen or more key points from your thumbnail sketch on your painting sheet and place light pencil dots at these points. They might indicate the horizon height, or the two ends of a roof of a building, the main corner of the building, or the placement of a tree

(see the example above). This assures an accurate start so that you will not end up with a boat or a building smaller or larger than you intended, or too far from one side of the painting so that you have more space than you can use at this point. If some other areas or objects give you trouble, simply plot a couple more points to work from.

Now you will find it easy to draw in all other items in correct scale and position. You have a painting guide and you are off to a good start. Many paintings which could have been good end up as disasters because the drawing was not true to the original plan and the artist, rather than start over, elected to go ahead and "think of something" to fill in extra space! Second guessing is painful.

The amount of drawing before painting will depend largely on the subject material. If buildings are involved, make sure the perspective is correct, then indicate large areas such as roofs, walls, and the like. If there are distinctly individual details that you want to preserve, such as dormers on a roof, log walls, where a shadow falls, or the angle of light, indicate these lightly. Rough in tree shapes for size, and position stone walls, fence posts, and such.

If boats or ships are involved, you will need to spend more time in drawing, since subtle lines of gunwales, bows, sterns, rigging, gear and many other details are important in correct portrayal. If you intend to use large figures or animals, you may find it helpful to draw them first on tracing paper to get correct size and convincing action. Then you can experiment as to the exact place to locate them in the painting. They can be transferred with a graphite sheet. (Do not use carbon paper since it leaves a greasy line which will not receive watercolor.)

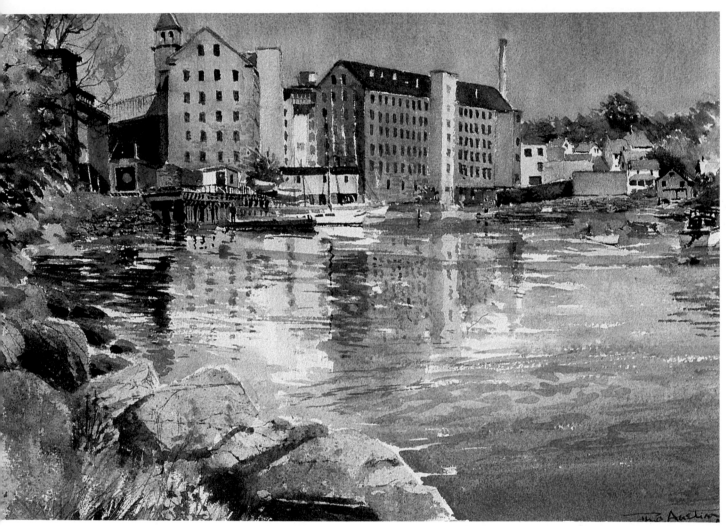

Old Stone Mills, New Market
13¹/₂ × 21¹/₂ inches

This painting was done in New Hampshire at the height of fall color, so that the warm color in the foliage contrasts with the cool gray of stone. Note the buildup of value at buildings' edges, use of shadow from buildings toward the left to create a dark-light axis in the river reflections. The lower right area of the water is deepened to fill the corner of the composition. The changing angles of reflections in this area change the flow of the river as well as strengthen composition.

6. The Painting Process

MIXING COLORS

The more rapidly you can assess color and create it on your palette, the more rapidly you can paint—a real asset in watercolor.

Recognizing what makes up a color makes mixing easier. It is possible to apply a value wash to your painting and, on the paper, do subtle color changes in that wash, making the painting more fluid, exciting, spontaneous and with more continuity—all qualities of a good watercolor.

One of the benefits of working with the limited palette I described in chapter 1 is that it allows you to learn the properties of the paint you're working with much more thoroughly.

CHANGING VALUE

Keep in mind that colors have both hue and value. Some colors appear very light, others medium in value, others dark. The value of a color can be changed, not by making the color richer—more intense—but by adding other color to it. A yellow which appears too light in a painting can be deepened by adding a little bit of orange. Adding a minute amount of ultramarine will deepen it further, making it slightly brown in hue. A little more blue added will make it deeper in value and slightly olive green in color, as yellow appears in shadow.

Another example: adding a very small amount of vermilion to ultramarine at the zenith of a sky in your painting approximates the darker blue seen directly overhead in nature. Green, with some ultramarine and vermilion added, becomes less bright in hue and darker in value, which is exactly what happens when a shadow falls across it.

In the series of seven panels shown here, the value of each color in the limited palette has been changed without changing the hue. Each panel was started with pure color, allowing it to blend into a graduated value of vermilion and ultramarine to create darker value. Note that each dark has become dominated by the particular color of each panel, not just a uniform dark. Practice with this way of mixing will allow you to paint with color while putting the emphasis on value.

Net Markers
15⁵/₈ × 11¹/₂ inches

This pile of net markers made an interesting color scheme, with gray shingles as a background and a yellow-green bush partially surrounding them. Note the loose wash character and variation in the window panes.

These two examples show two different approaches to controlling values as you paint. The band at top was created by first laying down a wash of neutral gray to establish the value. Then I dropped in bits of color—cadmium orange at the left, cerulean at the right—to give the impression of fall colors on a distant ridge.

To create the seven panels at the bottom, I worked the other way. First I established the hue, beginining each panel with a different pigment of the limited palette. I then changed the value by blending the pure color with vermilion and ultramarine.

Each of the seven colors of the limited palette mixes clearly with the next, remaining fresh and clear. This is important if you're to avoid muddy colors in your painting.

USING A NEUTRAL GRAY TO ESTABLISH VALUE

Since with the limited palette you plan first for value, then for color, you should establish the value by mixing ultramarine and vermilion to make colors of medium or lower value. Should you want a number of areas of different colors to remain uniform in value, you can mix the desired value with ultramarine and vermilion and add the approximate colors to reinforce each area. Thus your value will remain constant as you change color—an excellent way to pull the painting together!

The method of adding color after the value has been established is demonstrated in the example at top, which began as a middle value of neutral gray wash. A little cadmium orange added at the left end warms up the gray, while some cerulean added at the right end creates a cool gray. Then bits of cadmium yellow and orange, vermilion, alizarin, and viridian dropped into this wet wash give a hint of fall colors on a distant ridge. A few silhouettes of pines complete the illusion. The warmer gray and brighter colors on the left bring it visually closer, while the cool color on the right gives it distance. This has been achieved while keeping the value almost constant.

Before trying this method on a painting, do some experimenting on student-grade paper until you become familiar with what mixtures are required to get the values and colors you're looking for. The more you use the limited palette, the easier and more natural this way of working will become. You will find greater flexibility in handling values. Colors in the higher or lighter range of values such as yellow, normally will be used pure (diluted only with water), while slight deepening of value will be achieved with the addition of a little other color, as mentioned earlier. To repeat,

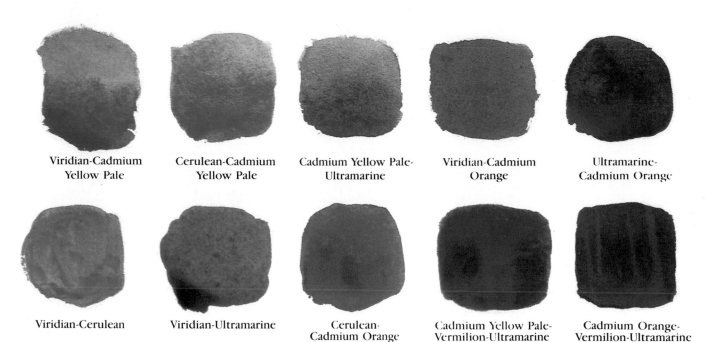

| Viridian-Cadmium Yellow Pale | Cerulean-Cadmium Yellow Pale | Cadmium Yellow Pale-Ultramarine | Viridian-Cadmium Orange | Ultramarine-Cadmium Orange |

| Viridian-Cerulean | Viridian-Ultramarine | Cerulean-Cadmium Orange | Cadmium Yellow Pale-Vermilion-Ultramarine | Cadmium Orange-Vermilion-Ultramarine |

Here you can see how easy it is to mix a range of colors with the limited palette. All ten are basically "green," but no two are quite the same.

This wash of earth colors consists of pure cadmium orange on the left, mixed with vermilion and ultramarine to create the darker values toward the right.

for middle values and below, you will wish to mix value first, then add color.

CHANGING HUE

The colors in the limited palette were chosen because they remain fresh and brilliant when mixed. The simple demonstration shown opposite page, bottom, illustrates the clear mix of each of the seven colors into the next. Since the cadmium yellow pale has no red in it, it mixes readily with either green or orange and remains fresh in appearance. Similarly, the green has no trace of red, so it mixes readily with yellow or blue, without losing brilliance. The ultramarine is a strong blue. It contains some red, which is useful, but for this reason, cerulean is also included in the palette since it has more of the character of sky and water, allowing lighter blues with no trace of red in them.

A few examples of mixing greens are shown top. In no case is viridian used as a pure color, only as an additive. Any variation can be achieved by changing the amount of each pigment used. The final two spots were achieved by establishing a value by mixing vermilion and ultramarine before viridian was added. In this manner, any kind of green, warm (orange added) or cool, can be created in as deep a value as desired.

The comment always arises, "But you have no earth colors in your palette." The wash shown at bottom demonstrates why they are not needed. Beginning with pure orange at the left, the varying wash is controlled by the addition of vermilion and ultramarine to create the whole gamut of earth colors, down to the darkest value.

Two reds are needed because alizarin contains blue and vermilion contains yellow. Alizarin is particularly useful for mixing with

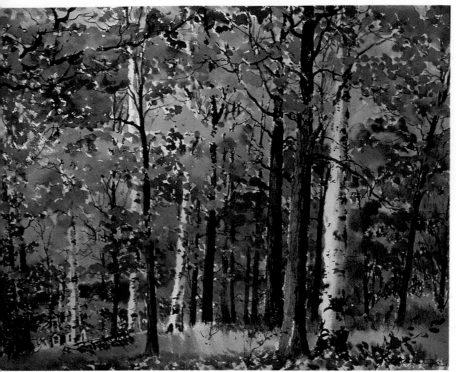

October in Ole's Woods
12½ × 29 inches

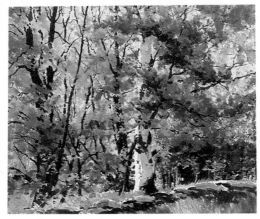

October on Collier's Ridge
21 × 29 inches

These two fall scenes show how the limited palette can be used to create very different color schemes. October in Ole's Woods shows the use of alizarin, vermilion, cadmium orange, and a bit of ultramarine here and there to deepen the value. The contrast of colors adds brilliance, as do the scattered dark trunks, white birches, and the dark distant hills, which also cause the color to stand out.

In October on Collier's Ridge, the alizarin gives a cooler look to the shadow areas of the foliage, while cadmium orange gives warmth to the light side of the trees. Again, dark trunks and limbs provide contrast.

blue for colors which tend toward violet, yet it is clear enough to mix with vermilion to create rich deep reds—such as the fall colors of maples and oaks. As for vermilion, it serves for mixing all the warm red and orange colors toward the yellow area of the spectrum. Vermilion also has another primary reason for being in the palette: it is an agent to create values.

Cadmium yellow pale is a clear, pure yellow which can be mixed readily with the oranges and the reds, yet can also be combined with the greens and blues.

Viridian is an intense green, again so pure that it can be mixed readily with yellow or blue. There are few occasions when this color will be used by itself, one such exception being to represent sea water with the light coming through it in a curling wave. Generally viridian is used as a "spice" to liven up a mixed green.

Ultramarine is an extremely useful blue, basic to both water and sky colors. Ocean greens are achieved with a mixture of ultramarine and viridian. Excellent blue skies can be painted with ultramarine and cerulean, beginning with

a very small amount of cadmium yellow pale added to the cerulean at the horizon, then passing through cerulean into ultramarine, then adding a small amount of vermilion to the ultramarine at the zenith. This sequence generates the feeling of the great vault of the sky. In addition ultramarine serves a second major purpose in this palette, that of being the second agent to create value.

Cerulean, the final color, is needed for blues which have no red in them. Also, since it has a slightly opaque quality, it serves to modify other mixtures and is a big help in making neutral and cool blue grays. I'll mention this use of cerulean from time to time for specific purposes.

You will find that a great variety of greens can be mixed with this palette. Cadmium orange and ultramarine produce olive green. Cadmium yellow pale and ultramarine make clear greens. Cadmium yellow pale mixed with viridian or cerulean produces spring greens. Thus by using two or more of these last five colors in the limited palette an uncounted number of greens can be created, allowing for

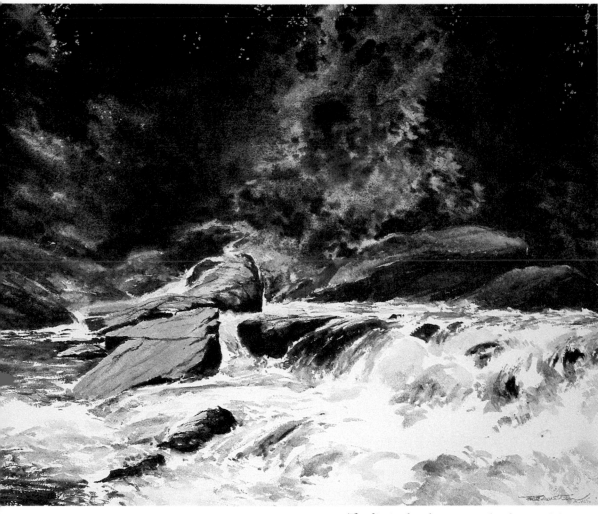

*The Turtle-Flambeau
Flowage*
21¹/₂ × 29 inches
*Collection of Employers
Insurance of Wausau*

*The limited palette can also be used for
cool, dark colors like those used here.
The rocks were done with a mixture of
ultramarine and vermilion with the red in
predominance. The dark areas were put in
with a very rich wash of this mixture.
Cerulean and a little vermilion created the
blue-gray shadows of the white water,
applied while the rocks were still damp so
that blending occurred in some areas. The
lighter greens were cadmium orange and
ultramarine blue with cadmium yellow pale
added in some areas. While this was still
moist, deep greens, made with a dark value
of ultramarine blue and vermilion, with
viridian added, were washed in and
allowed to blend freely with the lighter
greens. Finally, masking that had been used
to protect small light areas was removed
and those spots received a blue sky wash.*

a subtle flow of change.

At the top of this palette the variety you can
achieve—by mixing yellow and orange,
orange and vermilion, yellow and vermilion,
or yellow and alizarin—is endless. If you add a
little ultramarine experimentally to these mixtures, you will discover that you can mix all
kinds of browns, e.g., earth colors as demonstrated earlier. In addition you can achieve extremely dark values which will still be color, a
very important ingredient already discussed in
the use of value.

DEVELOPING A
PROCEDURE

There is no universally correct way to begin a
painting. Procedure is determined by the
physical circumstances, even in the studio.
Available time is a very real factor, particularly
late in the day. Approaching storms, changing
tides, a limited physical space in which to

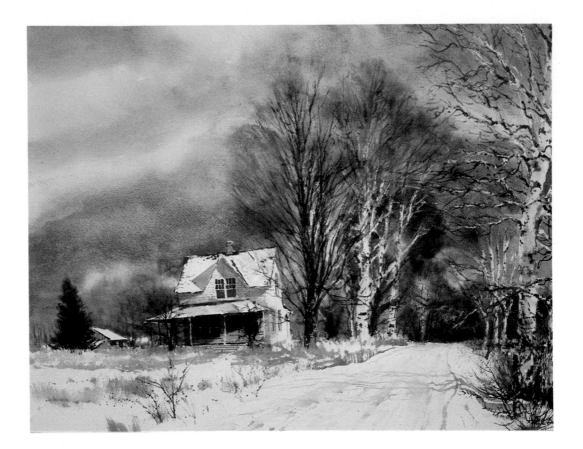

work, even unsympathetic or overinterested bystanders have bearing on this.

Rapid sketches and photographic references plus other notes are the best answer in some cases. This allows for much more complete planning in the studio before the final painting is executed. I am positive, however, that it is important to do as much painting as possible in a new and unfamiliar area before any attempt is made to study color slides, sketches, and notes, with the idea of doing studio paintings.

You may catch the mood of an area by observation, and get a strong emotional reaction to what you see, but in the long run you will have to round out your study through actual painting. You must know what colors are peculiar to that place, what atmospheric conditions exist, what sort of activities go on, what the people are like, what, if any, wildlife exists there, and what the tempo of life is. Then your emotional reaction will be valid.

To say, "I will always start with the darkest areas, or the lightest areas, or the center of interest" is to impose artificial restraints on the painting. Generally, however, I do plan to do the sky late in the painting procedure for a couple of very good reasons. If there is a noticeable hue or value in the sky, it is almost impossible to get the warm colors of trees and foliage completely fresh over a prepainted sky. There is always the danger that the objects thus painted will look somewhat reduced in bril-

A thin wash of cadmium orange, grayed slightly with ultramarine and vermilion, provided color for the weeds and grass. A gray wash of ultramarine and vermilion with a little extra ultramarine formed the clouds. The same wash, but with cadmium orange added, served for the blur of tree branches catching the light. The pattern of whites was planned, using birch trunks and snow on the ground and roofs. The darker values of the evergreen, window openings, cast shadow from the roof, and tunnel through the trees above the road were added last.

liance, or even "cut out" and placed on the sky. The second reason is that a definite sparkle is obtained by the necessity of painting around objects like trees, since in order to not run sky tones over them, bits of clear white paper will be left untouched. If trees are going to be darkly silhouetted on a light sky, as occurs in winter, or the trees are reduced to limbs and branches devoid of foliage, they can be done over a prepainted sky. However, even then it is well to leave larger trunk areas free of sky wash so that you will have complete freedom to introduce lighter, warmer colors if you wish.

Plan to introduce some areas of dark as soon as possible so that you can establish the span of values from dark to light. Try also to put in all the large, simple washes (other than sky) as soon as possible so that you can evaluate the amounts of greatest light needed without being confused by large areas of white paper. In areas to be left untouched, it is better to leave a little too much white than not enough, since it is easy to reduce these areas as you go along, but virtually impossible to reintroduce whites once they have been covered. State each value positively, as strongly as you feel it needs to be, on the first try. Correcting later can throw other values off, since all values are relative. Moreover, muddy color is likely. Indecision in a watercolor is as obvious as a billboard!

If shadow areas are changing rapidly, either lay them in at once, or indicate them lightly in pencil. Otherwise exciting features or details may be forgotten as the light changes.

When washing in a large foreground area, decide whether it should be a simple wet wash, an area of dry brush, or a combination of both. There are three kinds of edges: hard, soft, and rough or textured. Usually they all occur, in varying amounts, in different parts of a painting. If there is any motion in the foreground do as much as you can to suggest this with the direction of the initial strokes. Also, any texture or change in value suggesting terrain should be dropped in wet at this time, as well as any deeper value toward corners of the painting, if needed.

South Carolina Sawmill
14 × 21¹/₂ inches

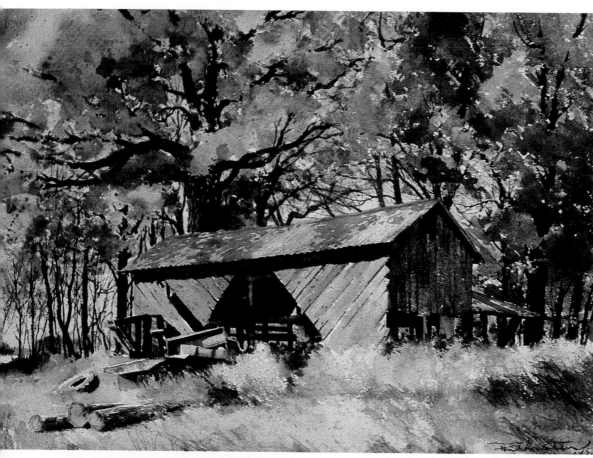

To create texture in a building like this sawmill, use strokes that run the direction of the boards. Direction strokes also give texture to the foreground. The simple foreground with bits of detail, roughly constructed mill, and surrounding oaks suggest a way of life.

51

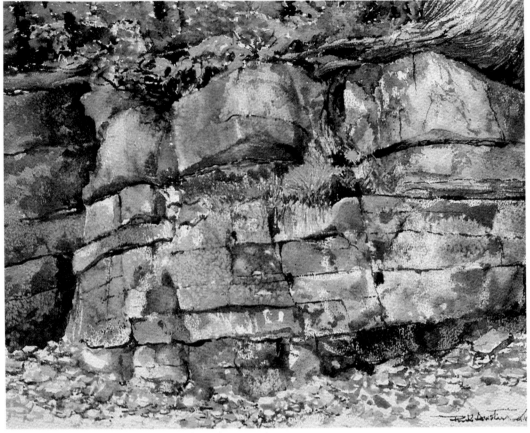

Fall Escarpment
21 × 29 inches

OBTAINING TEXTURE

Many textures can be obtained by using a knife or a brush handle in this damp wash. Your intention should be to say as much as you can, as simply as you can, in an initial wash. The less detail that needs to be added later, the fresher, more direct, and spontaneous the watercolor will appear.

The same procedure should be followed wherever possible in painting individual objects such as tree trunks. Values and hues are incorporated in the first wash. While the wash is wet, texture is added, using either a knife or a brush handle if necessary. The side of a building should receive vertical or horizontal strokes depending on which way the boards run, since even the slightest indication of brush strokes may suggest texture and construction (see "South Carolina Sawmill"). Any build-up of value toward one end or the other of a surface for contrast should be incorporated in these strokes. Any hint of changing color can be dropped into this wet wash as well.

As you go back to your palette for additional paint, frequently pick up bits of other colors so that there will be constant excitement and change in the washes you apply. Deep shadows coming from eaves, warm reflected light from the ground, cool light from the sky—all of these variations can go into a wall as you paint it. Again, hints of texture produced with a

Much attention was given to comparative masses of rock, texture, and value in this painting, which tells the story of the geology of the area and the persistence of tree growth. Large washes were applied for value, then additional values were added, and details were put in last.

brush handle are added to the wet wash. Any rocks in the landscape receive similar treatment.

After doing all objects such as buildings or trees which project into the sky area, decide how soft you wish the distant edges to be. If they are to be very indistinct, paint the sky leaving the lower edge moist enough so that you can come back with the distant hills, mountains, or woods, laying this wash in wet against the wet edge of the sky.

If you wish to have a more distinct line at the horizon, let the sky wash first dry completely, or nearly so. In some instances, a dry brush will help to make this edge more descriptive.

As you cover your entire sheet with these initial washes, do not stop to add details. When all is completed, then, *and only then,* consider what additional details are needed. Begin with the center of interest and complete it.

As you move across the painting away from the center of interest, reduce detail so that nothing will take away from that center of interest. It is always a temptation to add too much. Therefore, leave all finishing detail until the last. Invariably if objects are completed as the painting progresses some detail may be carried so far that there is no chance to make the main story stand out.

EXCEPTIONS TO THE PROCEDURE

There are, however, always exceptions to any procedure. You must be an opportunist. This was forcibly brought to my attention a number of years ago when painting in the Seattle area. I gathered my gear and went to Salmon Bay, where the idle fishing boats were moored. On arrival I observed what appeared to be an approaching rain storm. About to turn around and leave, I noticed a couple of ladies on a nearby dock busily painting. Not to be outdone, I hastily got out my paints and began. The sky was full of dark, rolling clouds and the masts and rigging of the boats were dramatically etched against it. The water had a dark, oily look. Wishing to record the sky, if nothing else, I hastily sketched in the forest of masts and rigging and plunged into painting the stormy sky, working carefully around all the

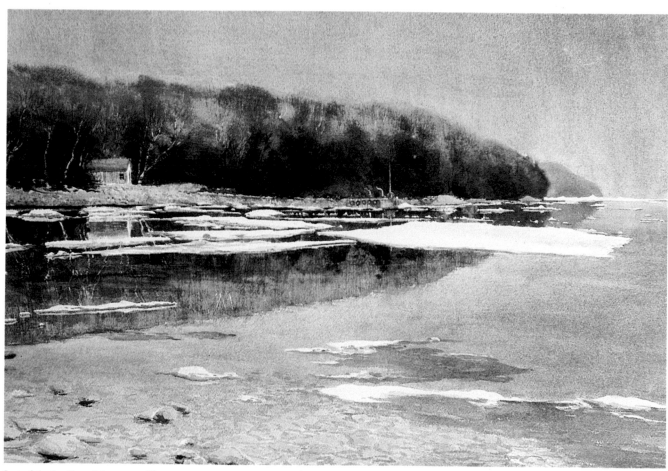

Last of the Ice, Garrett Bay
21 × 29 inches
Collection of Aid to Lutherans

Always carry your camera lest you miss an interesting moment or happening. I visit Garrett Bay frequently to see what's happening. This particular day the ice rafts drifted out in a matter of minutes. Exciting slides gave rise to this painting.

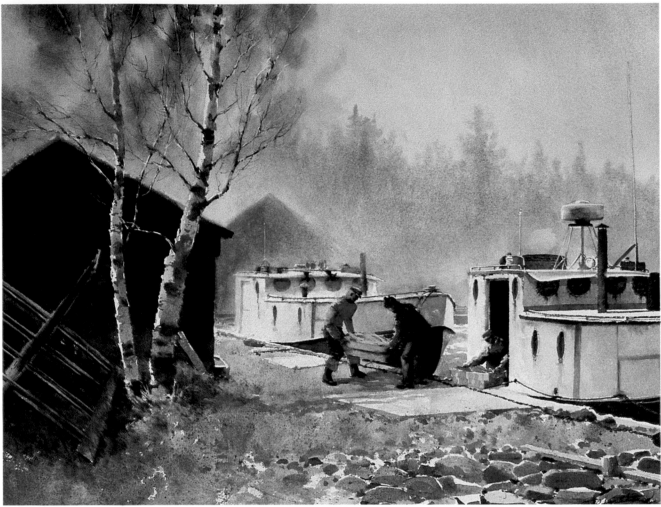

In Out of the Fog
21 × 28½ inches

uprights. Still no rain—so I rapidly penciled boat hulls and recorded the dark water.

Three or four hours later the sky was clear blue! Even though it was difficult to remember all of the earlier values, a successful painting resulted. It was loaded with the turmoil and the emotion caused by the approaching storm, but had I not captured the mood early in the painting, while the sky was so threatening, it would have been quite an ordinary picture.

At other times people or animals enter and leave the scene and it is necessary to hastily capture them complete with detail while there is opportunity.

On a March day when there was a light cover of snow, I was sitting high above the Mississippi River in the little river town of Chester, Illinois, to do a painting of "Mississippi River Country." Thinking about the theme, it occurred to me that what the river really needed to complete the story was a tug pushing a string of barges. Imagination, no! The throb of approaching engines brought into sight a tug and barges! Out came my Polaroid camera. As the tug reached a likely spot in the landscape, I took a black-and-white shot of it, and also made a hasty sketch. Studying my sketch and the photo for the proper wake and boiling

Fog added considerable glamour to this little spot on Sand Bay, and prompted me to use figures to develop a story. I completed the drawing first, then used liquid mask on small white areas, so that I could soak the sheet thoroughly and work wet-on-wet.

muddy water, I painted the river freight moving below in the yellow flood of the spring runoff. A plus mark for painting on location!

PAINTING "IN OUT OF THE FOG"

"In Out of the Fog" was prompted by the soft mystery of fog-enveloped fishing boats and sheds along the Lake Michigan shore. Introduction of fishermen unloading the day's catch added interest and a whole new dimension, suggesting the hazard of weather in a fisherman's daily work, the courage of the men who carry out their daily tasks regardless of weather. The implication is that the danger is past, with the boats safely in port. The painting is intended to suggest respect for these fishermen,

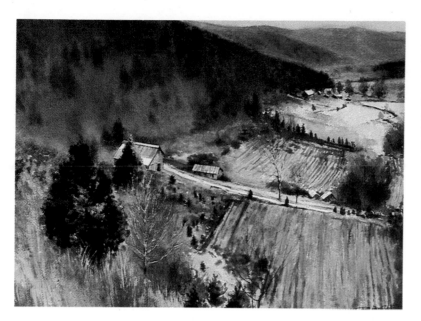

The method used for this painting was similar to that used for In Out of the Fog. *It was done wet-on-wet on a soaking sheet of 300-pound Arches rough. Color and value were worked carefully into the initial washes. Final details were added to the completely dry sheet. In the finished piece, the morning mist ties all the field patterns together in a subtle checkerboard of muted color.*

Renfro Valley Morning
21 × 28½ inches

and it will re-create their experiences for them as well. It communicates an awareness of and a reaction to the life around me—a most valid reason for doing the painting.

Here is a description of the procedure of this painting. After the preliminary drawing was completed, liquid mask was applied to the light side of the birches, the radio whips, radar drum, and light surfaces such as the tops of the boats, back rails and visors.

When this masking was completely dry, the full sheet was immersed in the tub for about five minutes until well soaked. Then it was stretched out on a sheet of wet metal (tempered masonite, glass, or Formica can also be used), to prevent rapid drying.

Work began with the background, the distant fish shed, and the purple-gray wash for the shape of the birch tops. The white vertical edges of the boats were blotted dry to keep the sky wash from flooding in on these surfaces. The deep red-purple fish shed on the left was also painted in with a "charged wash" (i.e., loaded with pigment) while the paper was moist enough to let it blur somewhat. Again the areas for the birch trunks were blotted, also to keep color from flooding them. The foreground was painted with some orange dropped into the wash at the base of the birches to bring this area forward. The drying rack for nets to the left of the birches was lifted out of the wash with a fairly dry brush and later finished when the paper was considerably dryer.

Now the painting was removed from the sheet of wet metal, the edges were dried with a blotter, and it was taped down on plywood with paper packaging tape so that it could dry faster and tighten into a stretch. The values on the boats were applied while the paper was still somewhat damp. Limbs and trunk detail were added to the birches. Some splattering of color with a loaded brush was applied to the foreground. Darker shapes were added to rocks in the immediate foreground when the paper was nearly dry.

The figures and the details on the boats were then painted in. Finally, when the paper was completely dry, the last little crisp details were added. The masking was removed and edges on the birch trees and boats were softened.

I always draw first, then use liquid mask where white areas will be small and difficult to hold, thereby enabling me to then soak the sheet thoroughly. I can then spend considerable time working "wet-on-wet" with all the large areas of a full sheet painting. Then by making a conventional stretch on a board, there is plenty of time to do areas which need to spread only slightly, before finally doing areas that need to hold detail. "Renfro Valley Morning" was also completed in this fashion.

Frequently the use of blotters eliminates the need for any masking of areas. I like the opportunity of working wet-on-wet and being able to combine it with later distinct wash and

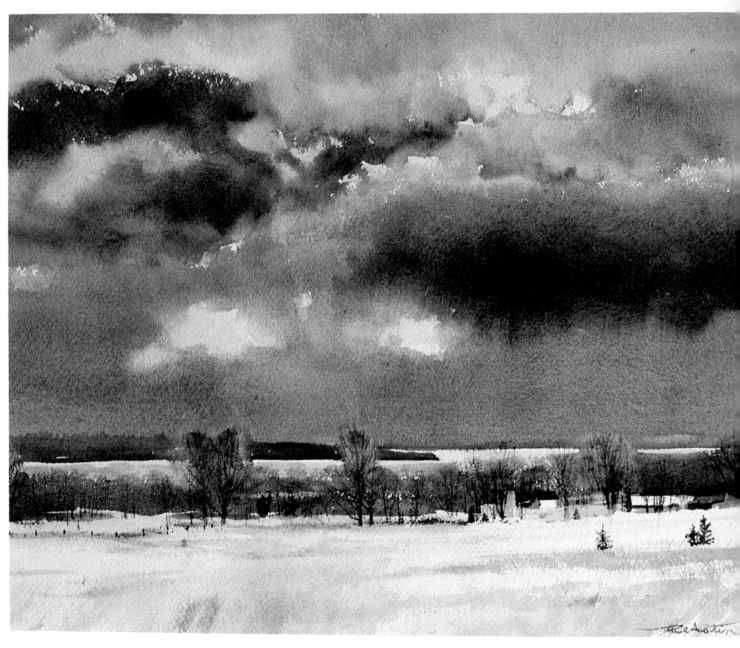

Storm Clouds Over Rowley Bay
11¹/₂ × 15⁵/₈ inches

These dramatic snow clouds were tumbling out over the bay. I dashed in the sky first, lest I lose it, then composed the scene below it, regrouping trees and farm buildings. Exciting skies like this are either won or lost in five minutes. The distant woods and nearby trees were painted together, using frequent brush-handle strokes in the damp wash. The foreground was done with a very light, dry-brush stroke, using a one-inch flat wash brush.

detail passages. Sometimes a limited area can be wet in preparation for wet-on-wet painting, but I find that a thoroughly soaked sheet will hold color where it is applied better than surface wetting, which allows more spreading of color.

In composing a landscape it is not always necessary to be limited by the exact appearance and arrangement of the subject you've chosen to paint. Some artists like to take photographs or make sketches on location and complete the picture in the studio. An advantage of working this way is that you are free to rearrange the various elements of your subject as you compose the picture in the studio.

When I am working this way from photos or studies made on location I first find a promising subject and then carefully study the area around it for elements that I can use—interest-

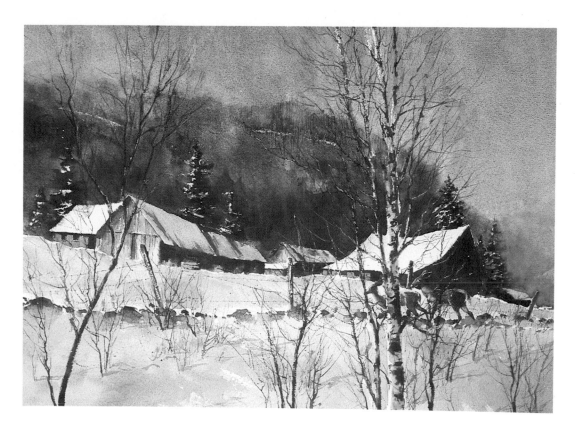

ing trees, rocks, buildings—then I put it all together in the studio. I make my sketches and take my photographs from different angles and points of view so that I will have a record of actual objects native to the area. Thus I maintain the feel and mood of the location when it comes to painting in the studio, even though I might change the direction of light, or the color scheme, or introduce figures and activities consistent with the scene but concocted from my imagination.

Whether you're working in the field or the studio you don't have to slavishly document exactly what is in front of your eyes. You are free to use your imagination and your good judgment to invent and compose. What matters in the end is a painting that stands by itself as a successful achievement.

WHEN CHANGES ARE CALLED FOR

Since watercolor is transparent, it is a revealing medium. Changes are very difficult to make. For this reason, it is usually better to redo a painting than to try to make extensive changes on the original. Because it is almost impossible to make an exact copy of a watercolor there will usually be something new, fresh, and unique every time a painting is done again.

The painting "Twilight Visitors" was based

The first time I painted this scene, I ended up with an area of bad wash in the right side of the sky. When I tried to correct it, things only got worse. So I finally decided to start over. To my surprise, the new painting was better than the original in every respect. I added a snow-covered wall and birch trees cutting the foreground. The background woods were raised, glimpses of snow were added to create a hill, and even the deer turned out better.

on photographs which showed two groups of farm buildings across the road from each other. A small watercolor of this scene made a good composition, so additional thumbnail sketches were made. The full sheet which resulted had an unfortunate area of bad wash in the right-hand area of the sky. Since 300 lb. Arches was used, it seemed possible to work it out. Everything failed; it got worse. I finally decided to start over even though many things in the original were unlikely to be captured again. However, I redrew the subject on a fresh sheet and began again and in the excitement of painting forgot the original and forged along on the new one. When it was finished, it surpassed the first one in almost every respect—even the deer looked better!

I am completely convinced that if you have a good subject and have not done it justice, even though you have a salable painting, you should

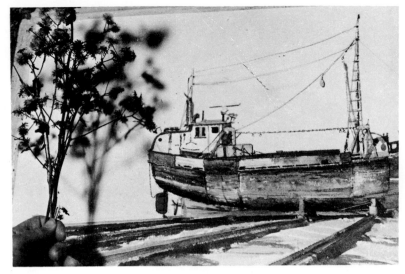

While working on this painting of a dragger along the St. Lawrence River, I used cast shadows to experiment with some possible additions to the composition before I committed myself to them.

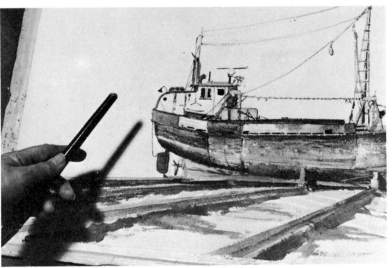

do it over until you have the best painting possible. Better to throw the first try into the drawer and do a second one than to be represented by a work with which you are dissatisfied. The back side of rejects can always be used for a new painting, or at least, to practice on.

There are times, however, when a painting can be corrected. In the painting "In Out of the Fog" discussed on page 54, I was dissatisfied with two of the figures. The painting was reasonably successful as a whole so I convinced myself that the figures would do.

The next day they looked worse. Starting with a brush and cleansing tissue, the figures and the whole bow of the second boat were gradually washed out, the sheet dried and reworked. This time the figures worked well with no evidence of change. To do this requires a good, heavyweight, hard-surfaced paper which allows for such treatment.

Sometimes it becomes necessary to add to a painting that you had thought was finished. A painting of an old boat sling was done on location on a cold, nasty, foggy day. Enamored with it, I submitted it for a national show, which it failed to make. When it came back, careful study revealed it had potential for a much better story. I started over and added a fisherman in

rain gear walking in with oars over his shoulder, but the second painting failed to have anywhere near the feeling of fog present in the painting done on location. With considerable trepidation I decided to work on the original, knowing full well that it might be destroyed. The figure was sketched in several sizes on tracing paper and experimentally placed in various locations until the best spot was found compositionally and storywise. Then I traced him into the original painting and began to carefully wash out any color which might be strong enough to show through the figure. This completed and the paper dried somewhat, the figure was painted in. The painting now contained a much better story. It is unwise to become so enchanted with your work that you fail to admit you can do better.

EXPERIMENTING SAFELY

There is a safe way to test additions to a painting while you're working on location. It sometimes becomes obvious that an object such as a fence post needs to be added for the sake of story or composition. Rather than paint them in wrong in the first place, take a brush handle, a pencil, or a twig, and drop a shadow on the painting where you were planning the addition. It is then easy to see whether the idea is valid and if so, the exact size and spot where the post should be placed. Similarly, if you are considering adding a tree or some brush, select a weed which will give a suitable shadow and use it to experiment. This answers questions without causing regrets (see the examples shown above)!

It sometimes happens that the foreground may need a dense shadow from an object outside of the picture plane to improve composition or direct attention into the painting. A piece of paper torn to cast the correct shadow can be used in a similar way to test the result before applying paint.

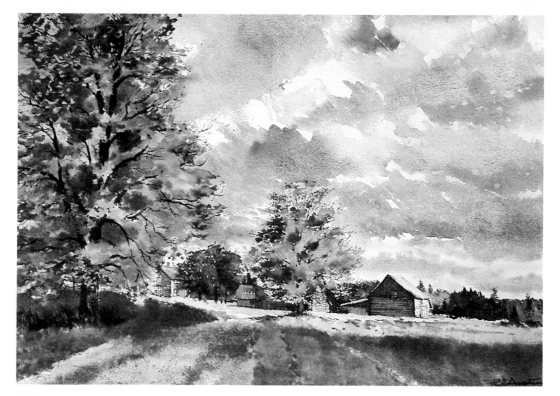

Fleeting Sun
21 × 29 inches

WHEN OPPORTUNITY KNOCKS

Sometimes accidental effects give a clue to improving a painting. Once when I was in the car painting some fields and a nearby grove of trees on a cold winter day, such a lucky happenstance occurred for me. The finished painting was not very exciting. I rolled down the window part way to get a little fresh air. The painting was lying on my lap in such a way that the light coming through the glass made a slightly darker value where it fell on the paper. It suggested a distant mountain seen through the foreground trees. The illusion improved the painting so much that I misted the area with my spray bottle to soften the color, and then I swept across the area with a big brush loaded with an appropriate wash. This made it into a good painting!

On a sunny day I was completing a painting with a simple foreground of a field with a roadway running back to a group of farm buildings. Broken clouds began moving in and a shadow suddenly fell across the foreground field, leaving the buildings in a patch of sunlight. The effect was so much better than my painting that I hastily misted the paper and added a shadow wash. Result: a greatly improved painting. Such chance circumstances can sometimes teach us new ways of thinking when we paint.

Many artists do all their painting within a small geographical radius, while others travel to distant areas to paint. If travel is your inclination, it can enrich your life and your work. This

Chance helped make this a better painting. I was working on location, and painted in the trees and foreground in the lightest colors. Then I added buildings and distant woods, then the sky. About that time, clouds suddenly darkened the foreground and left a ribbon of light around the buildings. The effect was so dramatic that I hastily darkened the foreground to match it.

is a very personal choice which depends on individual preference. If you choose to go farther afield for subject material, there are some things to keep in mind. Plan to stay in an area long enough to get the "feel" of the place so that your paintings will reflect a genuine understanding. Try to avoid the obvious things that everyone sees (and photographs). Get off the beaten track so that you see life as it is, not the facade sometimes presented to the public. Find the unusual views and activities that make the area unique. When you see or hear of unusual or relatively unknown areas or scenic wonders, plan your visit before everybody else gets there. You will find your painting trips far more rewarding.

From the beginning my wanderlust has prompted these kinds of painting adventures. My painting career has proved a magic carpet, allowing me to search out many new and stimulating places to paint, supplying me with a wealth of material and knowledge which brings me home to examine more familiar surroundings with a fresh eye and to paint with new enthusiasm.

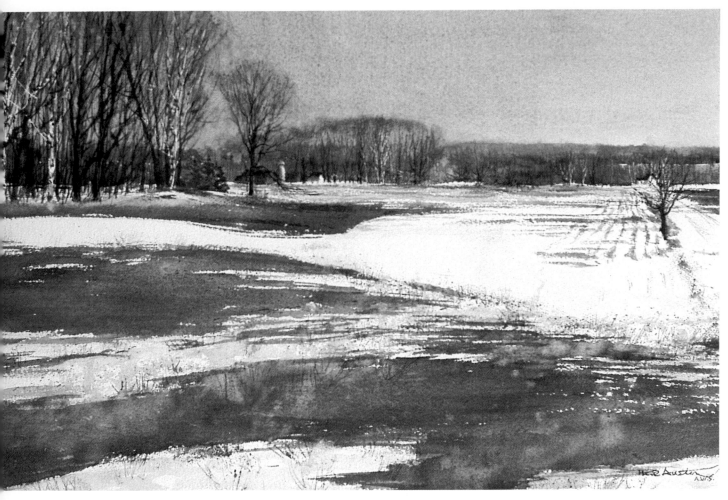

Pattern of March Fields
14 × 21¹/₂ inches

There is a stark beauty about the countryside before it awakens to spring. Snow lingers, making patterns of the fields. Woods carry a delicate pattern of limb filigree against the sky. Such times often supply the basis for interesting pictures.

7. Basic Landscape Techniques

We have discussed the thought processes in planning good paintings and have considered the various elements that enter into that planning: composition, patterns of motion, center of interest, positive and negative space, use of overlap, lost and found edges, increase of contrast, direction of light, and such. We have also considered the creation of color with the limited palette as well as the ways to create effective values.

It is now important for us to deal with the basic landscape techniques you can use to implement these ideas. Since a good watercolor painting should say everything as simply and directly as possible, beginning washes and strokes need to accomplish as much as possible. Individual objects or parts of the landscape need to relate to each other in the way light or shadow affects them not as single items, but as a group. You need to know, for instance, how to paint a continuous flow of light or shadow, and how to paint large shapes that actually imply character without using specific details. The shapes might be a group of trees, or a foreground that seems to come forward with perhaps slight ridges, clumps of grass, a scattering of weeds—all simply done. You

need to be able to suggest a pile or a wall of rocks simply but with character so that the final result is not a pile of bowling balls!

If you choose to paint water of some sort, it must be fluid and "wet," carrying spray or reflections that are not detailed, but suggested in the initial wash with little if any detail added later. If you're painting a rapid or a waterfall the motion must be implied by the use of directional strokes, value, contrast, and hard and soft edges, all contained in the early wash.

Examining the skies overhead presents the challenge of interpreting them with a dash and spontaneity that matches their character. You need to learn how to get depth and luminosity in your skies, how to imply their vastness, how to capture their motion, suggest their perspective, and indicate the weather and season—and to do it in a matter of minutes so that no artificial edges occur, changes in color flow naturally, and wetness is controlled. With this you also need to learn what paper will work best and how to use it: "surface wet," damp all the way through, or dry.

Learning these techniques will give you more freedom to capture moods, increase the variety of subject material you can tackle, and add to your joy in using watercolor.

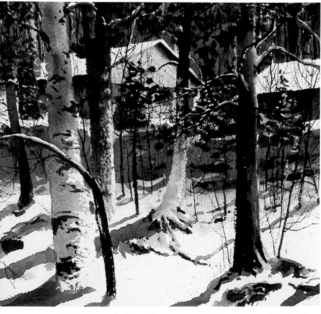

Full Moon in December
11½ × 15⅝ inches
Collection of Thomas
Zuchowski

At 4 a.m. I looked out at my neighbor's place bathed in light. That morning, using strong values of blue-gray and dark greens (ultramarine and vermilion with viridian added) I painted the remembered beauty.

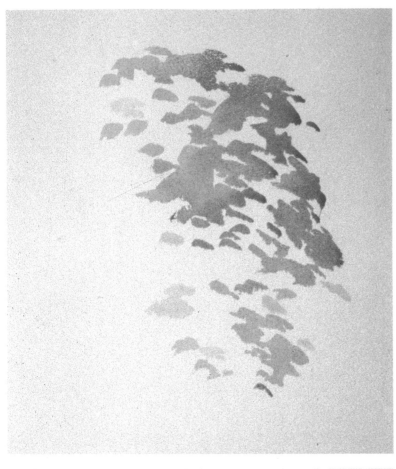

TREES

Trees have been celebrated by poets, writers, and artists since earliest history. They are worth special study. Early in my painting career, baffled in my efforts to paint trees, I concentrated on doing nothing else through all four seasons. Trees came to be individuals much like people, reflecting the life they had experienced. I now look for trees with characteristics all their own and seek the best way to interpret them. Here are some ways I find effective.

When painting foliage, look for the pattern of light and dark values. Then begin with the areas of most light, painting those areas only. Leave a dry surface on which to add the middle and dark values. In this manner you can hold any shape or definition wanted, and you can touch one wash to another for blending.

Step One. This spreading tree is a good one to start with. Its outspread top catches a lot of light, which is put in very wet on the dry surface.

Step Two. Now the second value is put in, again very wet, so that it blends readily in several places. Again, the paper is still left dry for the third value.

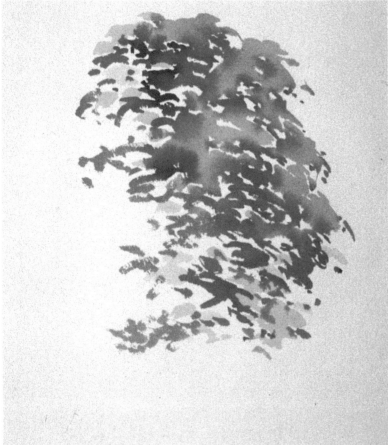

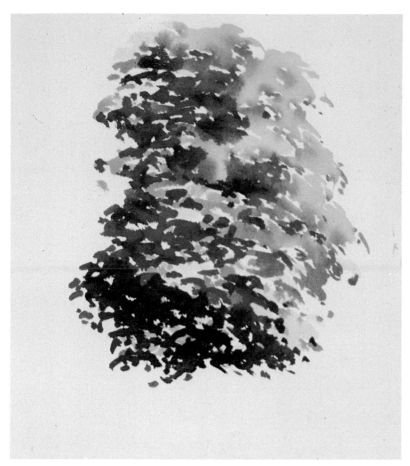

Step Three. The third value (in the case of a green tree made with a mixture of ultramarine and vermilion with viridian added) is painted on the dry surface and, like the second value, is blended in with spots of earlier washes.

Step Four. The trunk is added and textured with a brush handle. The branches are tucked into openings left for them and some of the surroundings are added. It's best if this can be done while the tree is still somewhat damp.

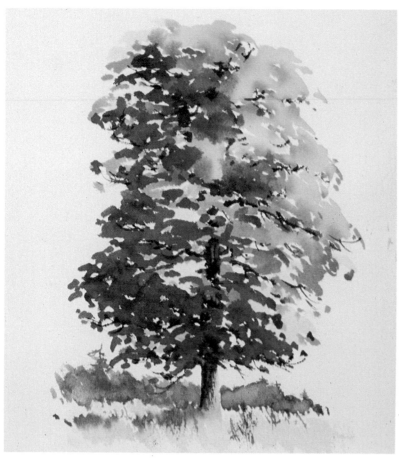

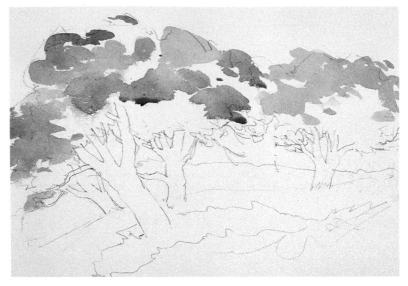

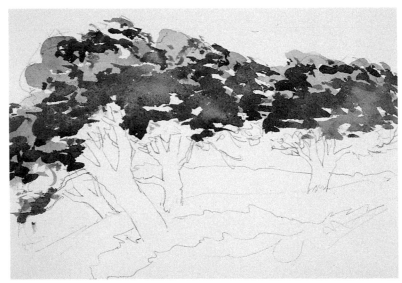

GROUPS OF TREES

If you are doing a group of trees, follow the same procedure by painting *all* light areas first as a pattern, then middle and darker areas. In doing this, even though you work on a dry surface, use a loaded brush so as to have wet areas of color and ample time to create flowing passages before the wash dries.

In painting trees (unless you wish to go into great detail) use simple areas of wash and considerable blending of values and then put in a few detailed leaves on the fringes of the trees and perhaps a few random ones at the edges of light areas. These leaves will be sufficient to identify the entire tree. Also study carefully the shape and limb pattern of each variety of tree so that it can be suggested by brush strokes— telling as much as you possibly can in the initial work. Studying and painting bare trees in fall and winter will help in this.

Step One. This is a group of oak trees on a California hilltop. The overall shape of the tree-tops is sketched, together with a careful drawing to suggest the character of the tree trunks. The lightest greens are painted first.

Step Two. The mid-value greens are added in the second step. At this stage you begin to model the trees, giving them the appearance of depth.

Step Three. In this final step the third value of foliage is added, pulling the tree shapes all together. The trunks receive texture in an initial wash, then further detail when dry. Branches and twigs are added to give character to the trees.

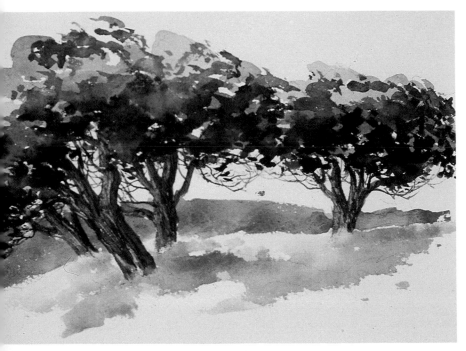

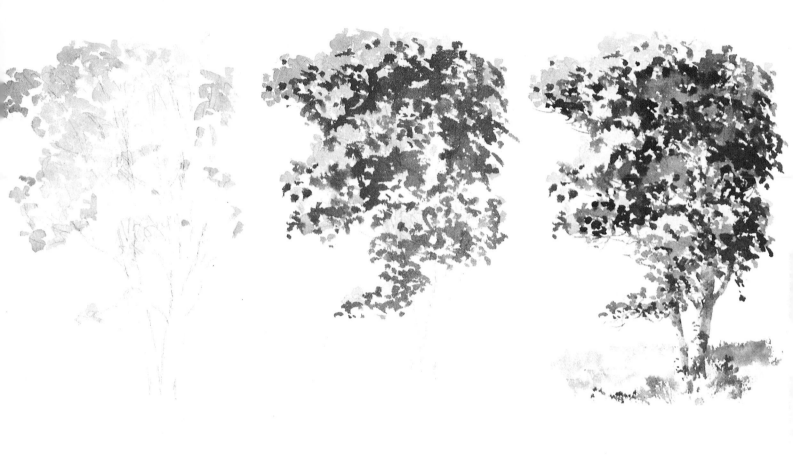

BIRCHES

Step One. When painting birch trees, pencil large shapes lightly, then paint light areas of foliage very wet, leaving all other foliage areas dry.

Step Two. Add the second value to the foliage in the same manner.

Step Three. Finally, complete the darkest area of foliage and add the shadow side to the trunk and branches. This trunk shadow can be a gray wash blued somewhat with a little cerulean, but as you go higher into the tree and also onto limb extremities, add a little cadmium orange and a bit of vermilion to create a warmer shadow on the trunks and even a rusty color on branch ends and smaller twigs. This is characteristic of birches.

Now add the dark markings to the birch trunk and limbs. Keep these darks scattered with no regular repeat of size or position. Frequently the darks will appear as a saddle in a crotch where a limb or a side branch begins. These darks remain where a limb has once been as well. In planning the surroundings for a birch, employ darker areas or different hues in some places to define the white edge of a light trunk or limb. In other places deliberately allow lights to create a lost edge—similarly with darks against the shadow side of the trunk. This gives a freedom and looseness which causes the tree to be part of the landscape. In the late winter and early spring these limbs and twigs become almost alizarin in color from the forming buds. A birch tree devoid of leaves will require a shape done in the sky while wet with a light gray wash dominated with alizarin.

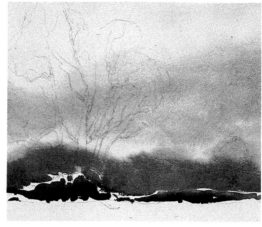

WILLOWS

Step One. I began with a little watercolor sketch of a winter swamp with a cluster of old, battered willow trees. In the first step the sky, distant woods, and brush clumps were washed in.

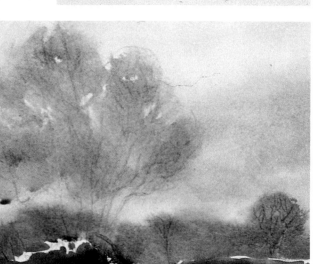

Step Two. While this was still damp some darker wash was dropped into the sky where the shape of tree limbs, branches, and twigs was to be. A little more was added for a tree clump or two in the distance. While these additions were still damp some brush-handle work gave limb texture to the wash.

Step Three. In the next step tree trunks and branches were painted in, feathering out into this wash. Finally a few foreground accents and weed stalks suggested atmosphere. This is a very good way to create winter trees.

A second method is to paint in the trees and then soften the limb ends while they are damp and if necessary, add a little wash for the tree form. This allows a little more control but sometimes does not have quite the freshness of the method here demonstrated.

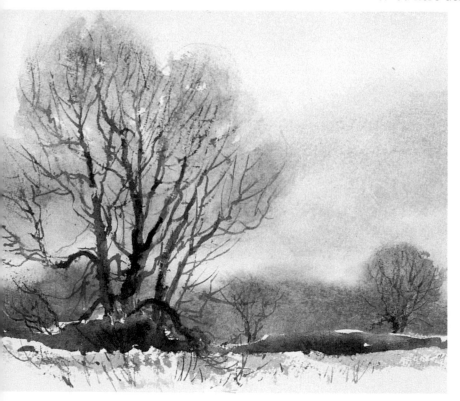

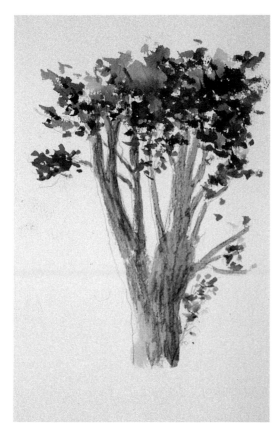

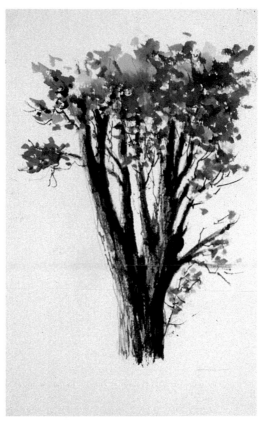

TRUNKS

Step One. The next demonstration shows the creation of bark texture with wash and brush-handle work. Note the trace of brush-handle work in the initial wash.

Step Two. A second darker wash also carries similar texture. (Remember, when applied to a wet wash, a darker line is achieved, but when applied as the wash begins to dry, lighter marks appear.) A few darker brush strokes applied while the paper is still slightly damp finish the texture of this maple trunk.

The trunk texture really adds to this center of interest, an old stump that I zoomed in on. Masking kept the flowers untouched until the stump was completed, and some masking was used for distant flowers as well. A loose background and sky were washed in.

The Ancient Stump
11¹/₂ × 15⁵/₈ inches
Collection of Mr. and Mrs.
John Rosberg

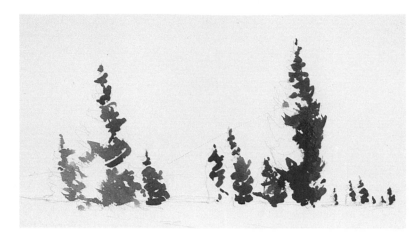

CEDAR TREES

Step One. In painting cedars begin with the light side of the trees, using a warm wash of cadmium orange and viridian. Next mix a darker value, using more viridian and some ultramarine with the orange, and apply it while the first wash is still damp so that considerable blending occurs.

Step Two. Following this, mix a dark value with vermilion and ultramarine, adding viridian until the dark becomes a proper green. This, too, is added while the second wash is still somewhat damp. This time keep this darkest dark in the center of the trees, so that even when it blends with the lighter wash there is a cylindrical feeling to the tree forms.

Step Three. Lastly, if more softness is needed, use the spray bottle for a burst of fine mist over the trees, allowing the outer edges to blur slightly. (It might be well to practice this on a few sample trees before you try it on a painting—lest you wash away a good area.)

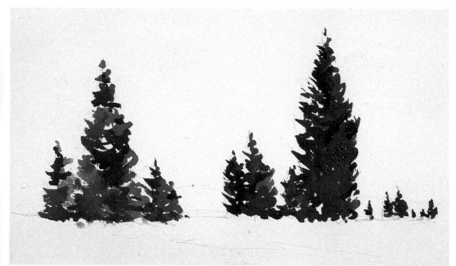

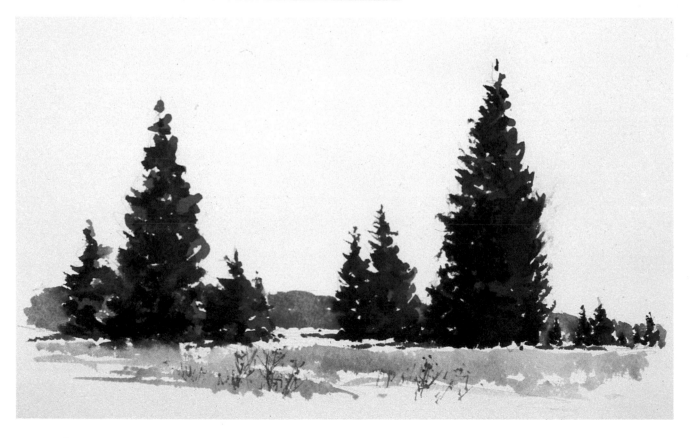

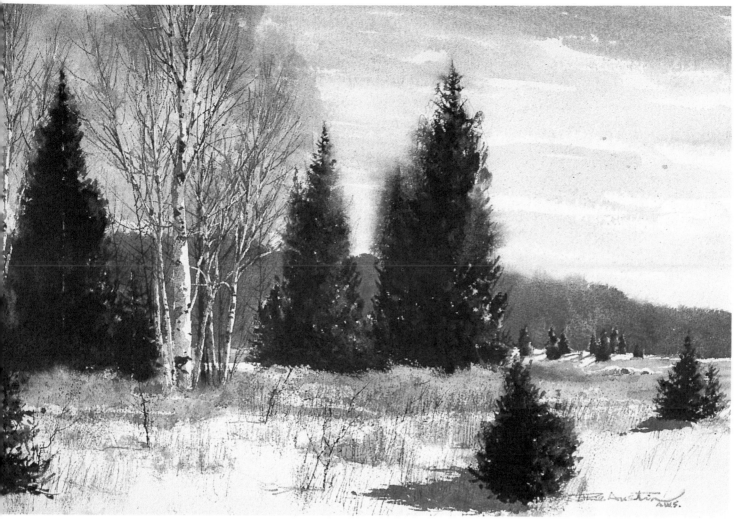

This painting makes use of the techniques for painting cedars and birches to capture the mood of the day.

The Quiet Time
14 × 21½ inches

PINE TREES

Pine trees have individual character as you can see in the illustration at right. It is always a question as to what is the best approach. The pine on the right was done with an effort to keep control, so the limb areas were moistened with clear water. After the glisten was gone, I washed in the light areas, then mixed a darker value and added it while the first wash was still damp, allowing considerable blending. Then, when dry, came the details with a small brush.

The two trees on the left were painted rapidly, again following the procedure of light color first, then darker values. Immediately after laying in these washes, I sprayed the trees with a dash of mist so that edges blurred considerably. (If working in the studio, a 1200-watt high speed dryer can be used to arrest the spreading if it seems to be going out of control.) After this was dry, I did trunk, limb, and branch detail with a small brush. This second method is a good one. It takes practice, however, to avoid getting too much moisture on the trees, thereby losing character.

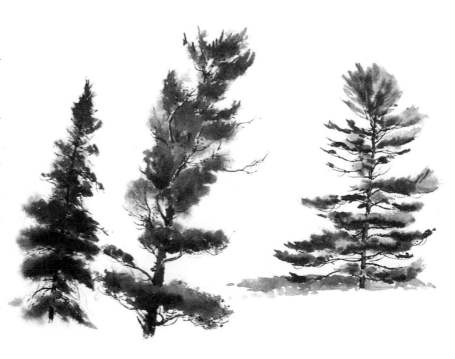

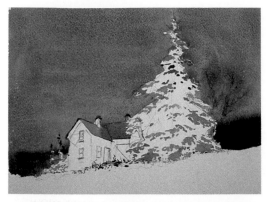

EVERGREENS IN WINTER

Step One. When you paint winter evergreens with snow on them, put liquid mask on the snow areas first so that you can paint the tree freely and still hold the snow areas. The first step shows this with masking on the limbs (also some on ground area and white areas on the little building). The sky was painted, staying clear of most of the tree area.

Step Two. The second step shows the evergreen painted in and misted with spray to soften it.

Step Three. In the third step the liquid mask has been removed and an important addition made. I almost never leave a masked-out area as it appears when the mask is removed. In this case, a second value was added for shadows and the weed stalks across the white areas left in the foreground. Unless this is done, the white masked areas will look artificial—like cutouts.

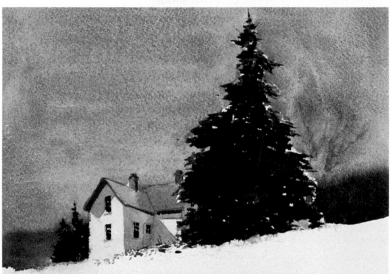

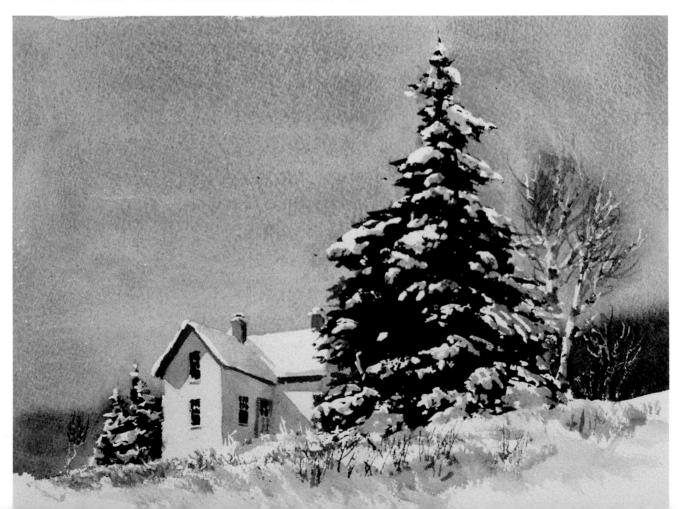

FOREGROUND I

Step One. In the first step I used a full brush of thin wash on Arches rough paper. A diagonal stroke, using the full side of the brush with a light touch, allowed some paper to show through to increase texture.

Step Two. While this was moist some horizontal strokes of darker wash were laid in and a brush handle used to increase texture, following the direction of the earlier brush strokes. Finally, after this was dry, I added a few blades of grass and weeds in places. (This should be done very sparingly, since a few strokes will "read" for the whole area.)

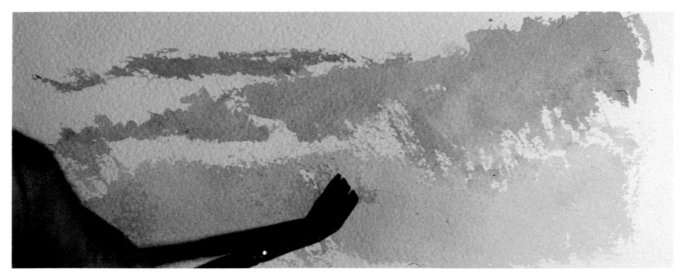

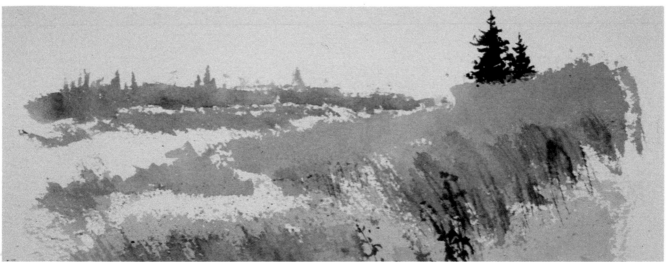

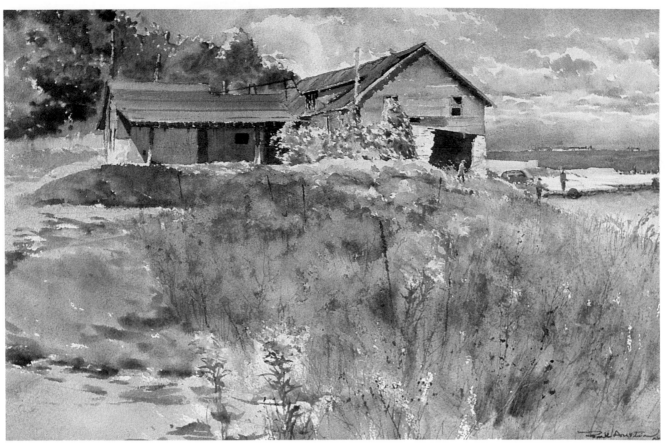

The foreground, approximately two-thirds of the painting, is handled very simply so that it becomes negative space, leaving the old mill the center of attention and helping point out the figure passing the dark opening.

Fishing at the Old Saw Mill
14×21½ inches

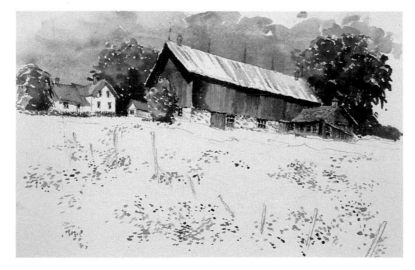

FOREGROUND II

Step One. A farm landscape has been started and the foreground spotted with liquid mask to provide for pink and white weed blossoms and fence posts.

Step Two. Now the foreground has been washed loosely with varied shades of green and color for the pink flowers. When this is completely dry, a pickup is used to remove the masking.

Step Three. The third step is to add brighter spots of pink, some of it splattered with a brush for a "loose" feel. Weed stems and detail in fence posts complete the painting.

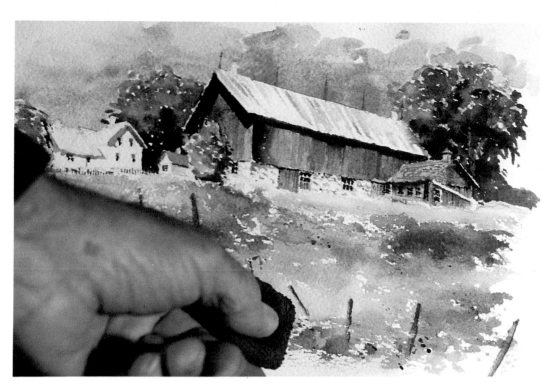

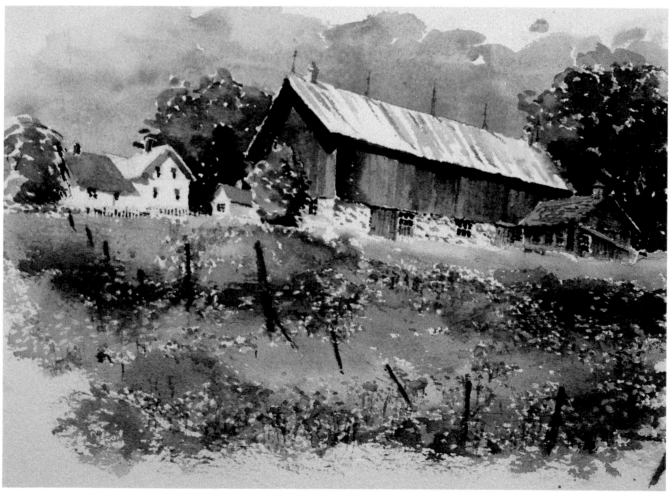

ROCK WALLS

Step One. This first rock demonstration is a wall of field stones piled up with little effort to fit stones together. I first made a careful drawing, then washed a shadow area on the entire wall as one piece, varying color and value slightly in some areas. The texture was achieved by sprinkling some salt on this wet wash.

Step Two. In the next step I mixed a darker wash and again went the whole length of the wall, molding each stone a bit more. At this point the foreground was worked into the bottom of the wall, which was still damp so that color would flow slightly, losing some of the edges. Some old mullein stalks helped to break up the wall so that its compositional pull toward the distance would be slowed.

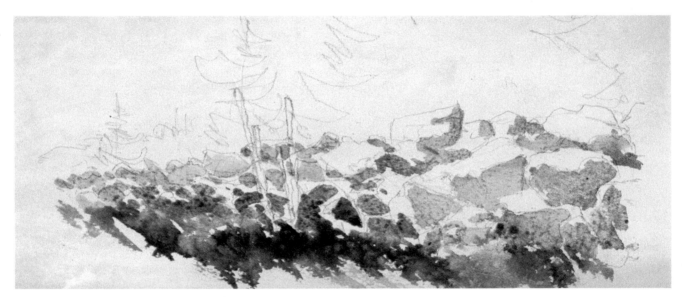

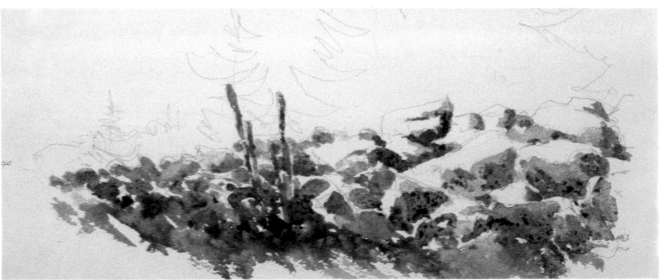

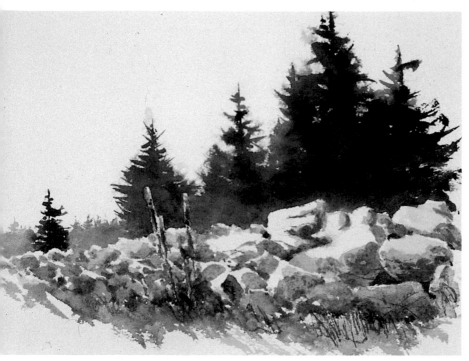

Step Three. Dark trees were added beyond the wall to etch the top of it with light. The salt was still working on the washes of the wall. This is something that can't be hurried. Drying the wash with a dryer would stop any further texturing of the wash by the salt. Value relationships could now be compared. A third value was applied to the wall. Final touches included putting in seams and dimples in the limestone and adding a few dark pockets of shadow on the nearer part of the wall. The final result then carried well, as the greatest amount of light and dark were concentrated where the most detail was—the center of interest.

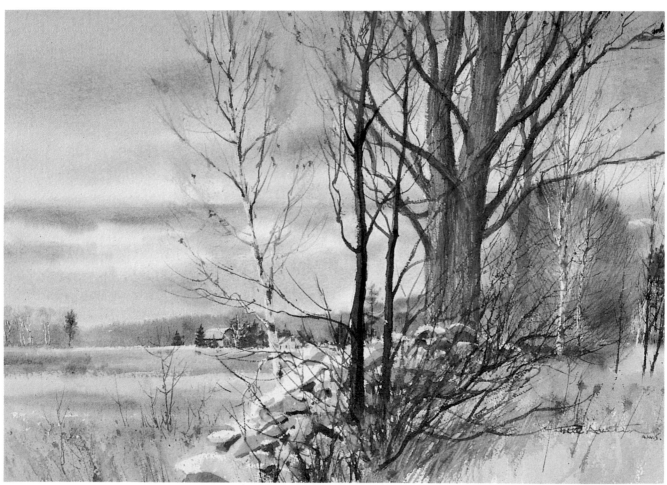

The rock wall works with the varying dark and light verticals and the horizontals of sky, clouds, and grass to make a grid of the emptiness of fall, the very bones of the landscape.

The Last of Fall
13³/₄ × 21 inches

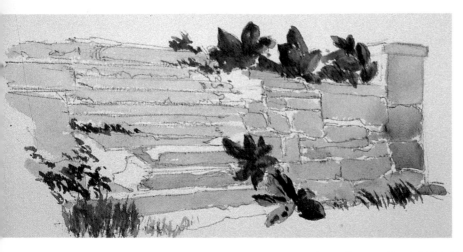

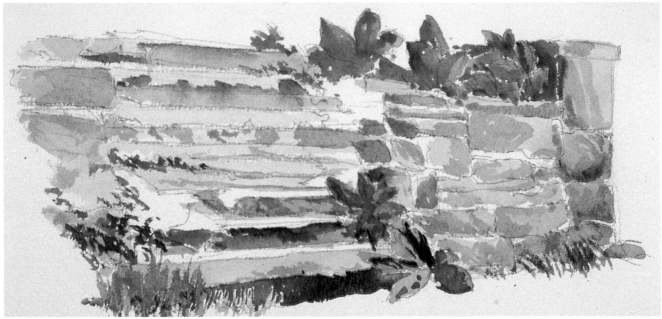

STONE AS MASONRY

These dilapidated stone steps are part of an old stagecoach stop at Hilt, California. They make an interesting subject to demonstrate painting of rocks used in masonry. I began with a careful pencil drawing, making sure the perspective was accurate. The old burdocks were included to explain the crumbling steps.

Step One. A light wash was laid over all the stone areas, leaving white paper for mortar joints, as well as light-flooded surfaces such as the steps. Cadmium orange with a bit of ultramarine and vermilion added gave the color of the old limestone. The weed growth and scattered grass were indicated with a mixture of cerulean and cadmium orange, producing a warm green with some bluish traces from the cerulean.

Step Two. The value of the wash used for the limestone was deepened and used in slightly varying values as the different areas of stone were washed over. This is easily done if, each time you go back to your palette, you pick up a little of a different color or a variation of value to give individual character to the stones. This procedure brings out the mortar joints a little more strongly. The front edges of the stone steps were deepened to emphasize the lighter surfaces of the treads.

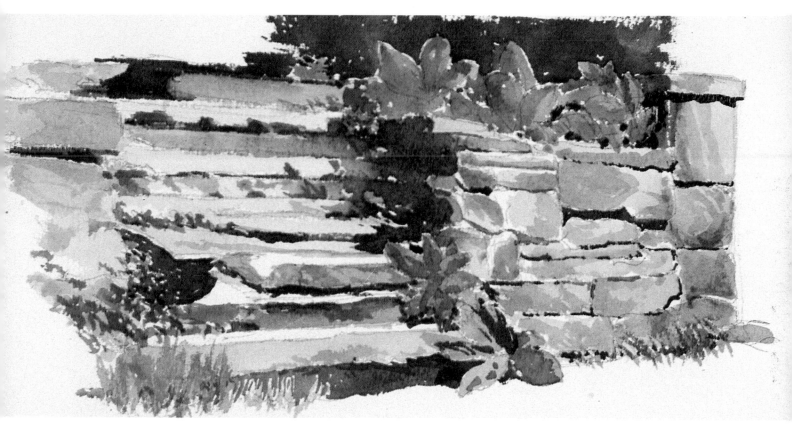

Step Three. A dark mix of ultramarine and vermilion was added for cracks and shadows from overhanging surfaces, cast shadows from weed leaves, and holes where stones were missing. This delineates the surfaces. A few darker accents molded the rock surfaces further, while still maintaining the overall look of the stonework. The vignette shape concentrated the interest. A final shape of dark etched the top weed leaves and caused the steps to stand out better by contrast, making the remaining whites sparkle.

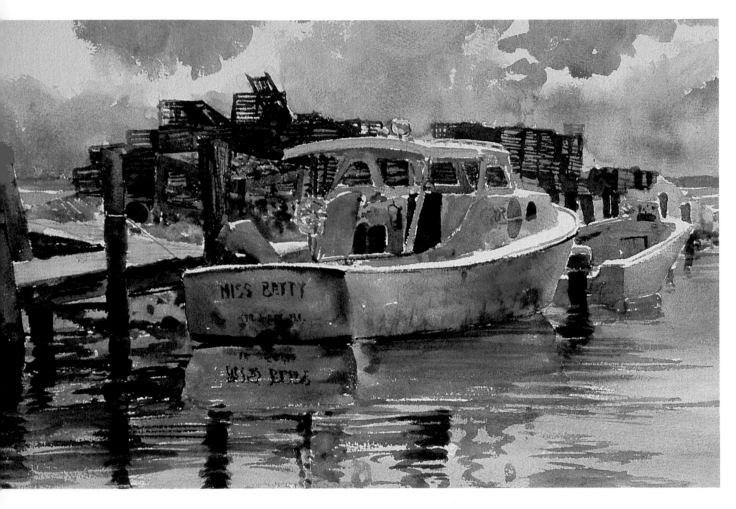

90°, Sugarloaf Key
14 × 21½ inches

Everything here adds up to suggest a hot summer afternoon. The reflections indicate clear, almost still water. The strong shadows and surfaces swept in light from a sun directly overhead suggest the heat. The dark silhouette of lobster traps stacked against the sky adds to the activity of the scene.

REFLECTIONS

Step One. This little sketch demonstrates how to create reflections. In step one the surroundings of the pond, a grassy field, an evergreen, some birches, a cottage, and a shed were painted. Note that the grass at the far side of the pond is darker than the grass in front of it. This could have been reversed, the idea being to have a light area of water against a darker background and dark water against a lighter area of surroundings.

Step Two. Now the reflections were painted into the little pond. Objects close to the far edge reflect completely—like the evergreen and the fence posts—while only the higher parts of objects farther away show. Anything low or distant will not be reflected.

Reflections duplicate any action—but in reverse, like a mirror. Thus a fence post that is upright reflects a straight line, whereas a post leaning to the left will also mirror a post leaning to the left. A few horizontals stroked in will flatten the surface and give perspective. If there is any breeze, images will be fractured rather than sharp. A stroke or two with the brush handle while the wash is drying will add a light ripple which will increase the illusion of a flat, wet surface.

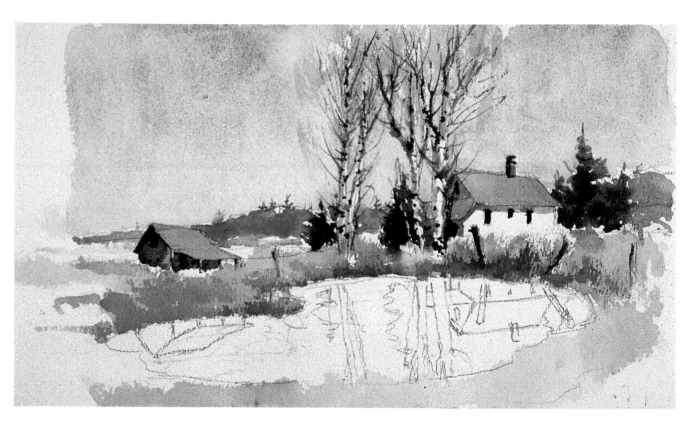

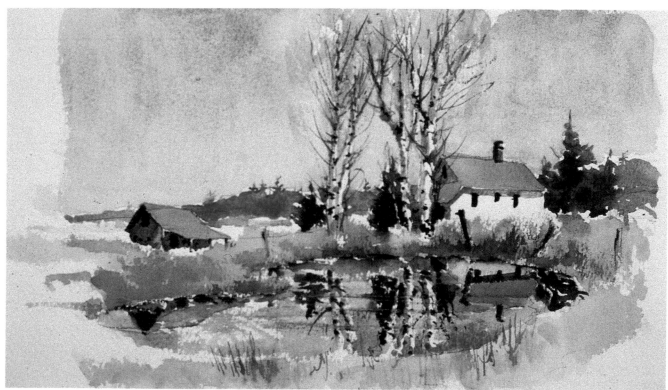

79

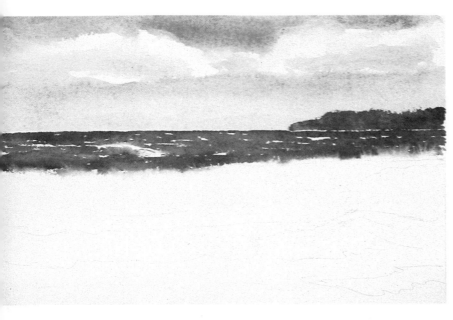

INCOMING WAVES

Step One. Determine the kind of day you wish to portray and paint the sky first, because this will control the color value of the water. In this case the waves are large, denoting wind, so leave some scraps of white as you paint the distant water. As you bring this wash nearer the foreground, wet an irregular edge for the top of the first large wave, and bring the wash to it, leaving a blurred edge of spray

Step Two. Moisten the bottom of the large wave and paint to it as you indicate a deep shadow under the curl. In doing this, leave a few areas of the wave edge dry, but let others blur so that there is a combination of soft and hard edges. The wash in front of the wave is characteristically lighter in value and more green in hue.

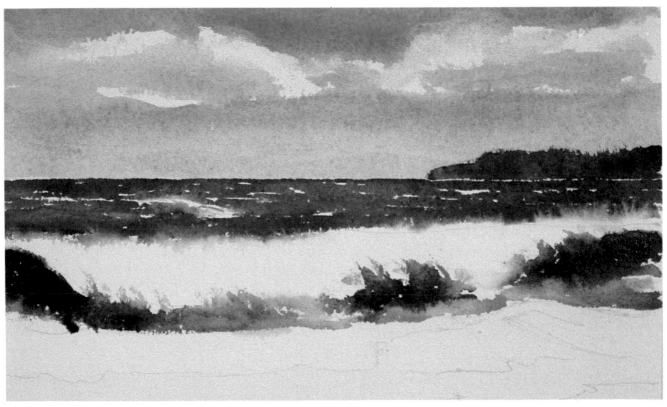

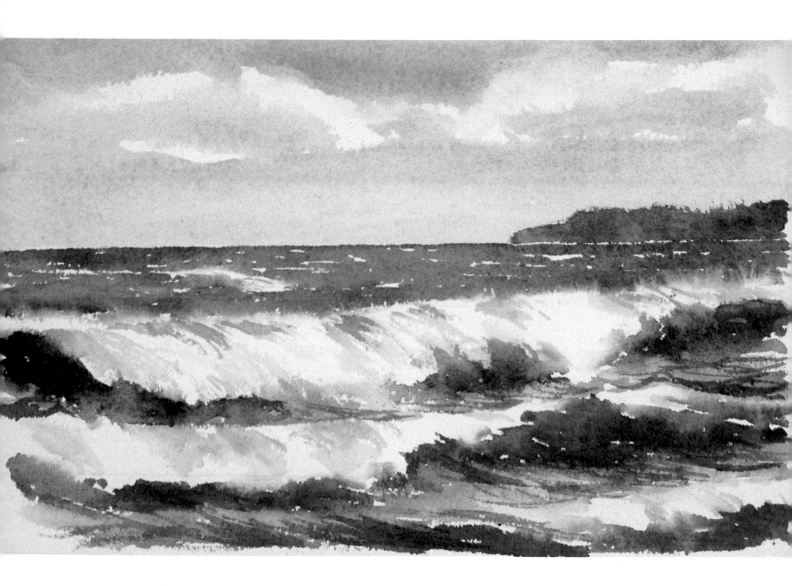

Step Three. Repeat the procedure for the second wave and the scrap of foam in the lower right. Use long curving strokes, convex in some areas, concave in others, to indicate the swell. If you plan to bring the water all the way to the shore in the foreground, add a little orange to your wash for warmth to indicate color from the bottom shining up through the shallow water. The turmoil of water in front of the last wave can be shown by long, flat, oval strokes that change color slightly here and there and leave quite a bit of white paper showing.

Finally, use a flat brush with a light wash of pure viridian and follow the curve of the breaking waves to indicate light coming through. Soften some of these strokes in places with pure water to blur them slightly.

In painting a body of water, the sky, as mentioned earlier, is important since a clear sky or one with scattered clouds, as appears here, will produce a deep blue color to the water. Ultramarine with some viridian added will do this. The deep value beneath the curling wave includes viridian, plus some vermilion to create the dark colors. If the sky is overcast, ultramarine with cerulean and vermilion will give a blue-gray water to match it.

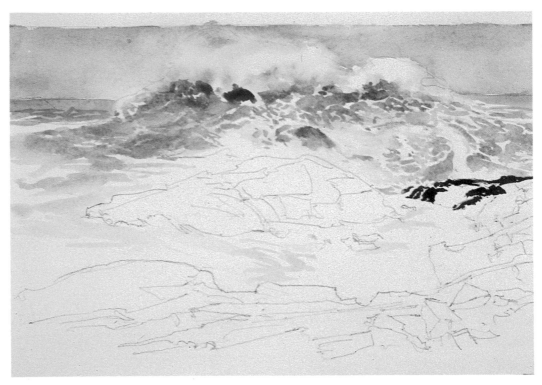

BREAKING WAVES

When painting waves breaking on a reef, rocks, or a dock, you can give them scale by showing spray breaking up across the horizon.

Step One. In this demonstration, the sky was painted first with a pale wash against a wet edge for the top of the spray. When this was dry, the distant sea and horizon were put in, again working to a wet edge for the flying spray. This turmoil of the wave was painted with plenty of color in the brush so the wave would stay wet. As the strokes were applied, the color was varied, more green in one stroke, a little more blue in another, to create surfaces that catch light differently. When this was finished, a slight misting with a spray bottle was applied to soften the effect. A few strokes of a light gray-green wash in the foreground gave action in the water and reduced the white areas so the crest could dominate as the largest pure white.

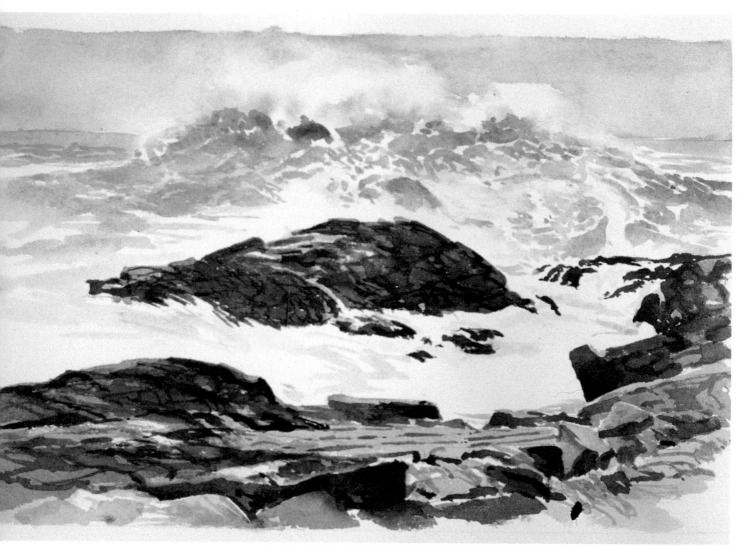

Step Two. The rock surfaces were painted much as in the demonstration for rocks shown earlier—light areas first, then darker areas, but working on the entire surface, not piecemeal. Finally, an extreme dark was mixed with ultramarine and vermilion and details were added to the rock surfaces.

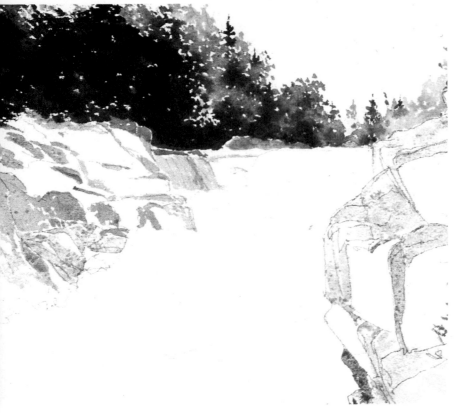

RAPIDS AND WATERFALLS

This is a subject which should be done on location if possible. If you work from slides or photographs the temptation is to paint every little detail "frozen" by the camera. Painting on location presents the challenge of doing a composite of the characteristic action, creating life. It is well to study waterfalls, rapids, waves, or spray for some time before commencing to paint. Then almost from memory, paint rapidly with the minimum number of strokes possible.

Step One. First, the subject was sketched lightly and all the light areas of the rocks painted with a very wet wash of varying color and value. Salt was sprinkled into this wet wash to create texture on the rock surfaces.

Step Two. Middle values were put in, then dark values, which were allowed to blend slightly. Salt was again added to the wet wash.

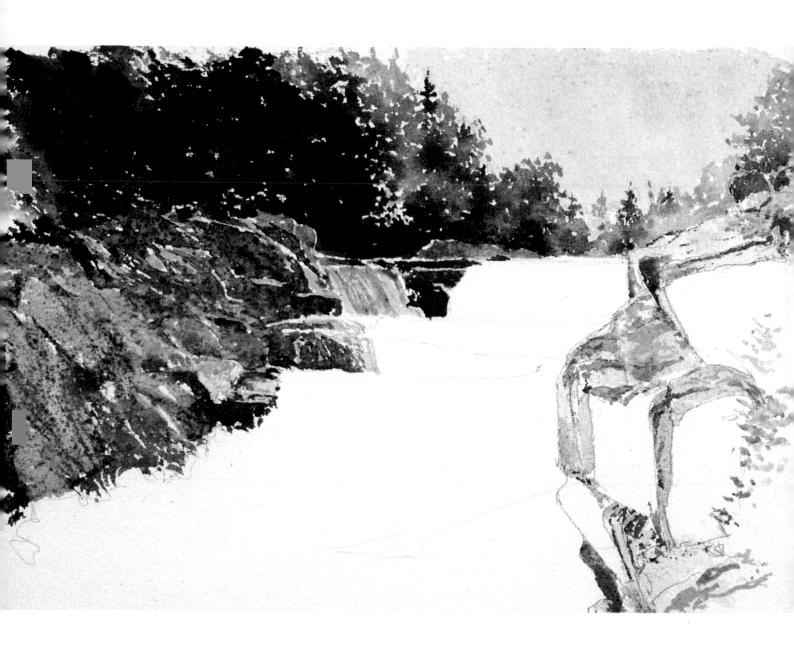

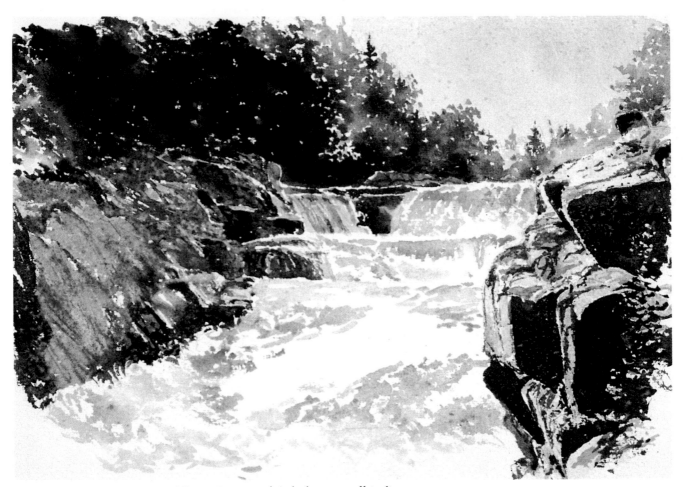

Step Three. Because the darks were all indicated, the values for water were easy to gauge. Edges of the white spray were dampened, directional strokes of blue-gray (very light) curved to follow the flow of the water, blending out into the damp edges of spray. These were slightly deepened in value where they approach pure white areas of foam at the bottom of falling water, not on the flowing slope.

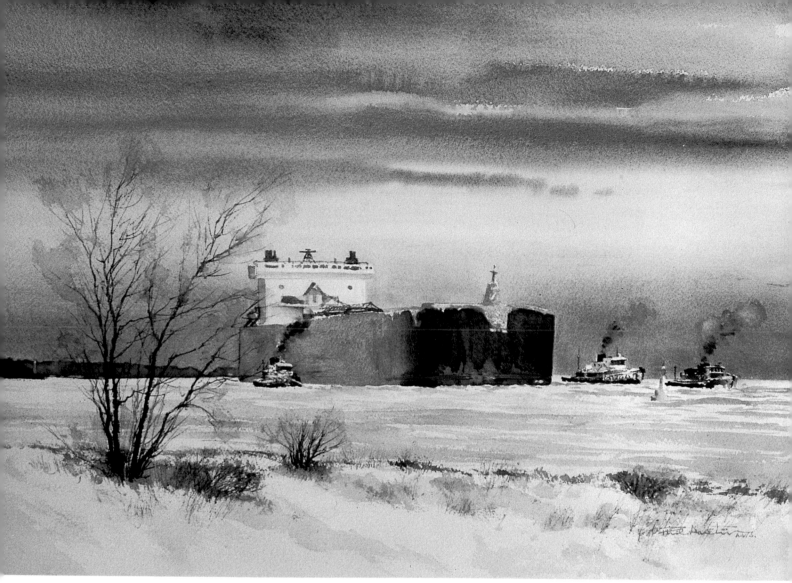

Breaking Ice for the Edwin Gott

21½ × 29 inches

The mood here is that of a cold winter morning. The sky was glazed first with a warm wash of cadmium orange and vermilion toward the horizon. Later the lavender clouds were added to the redampened sky. The tree branches and the slanted smoke of the tugs help suggest the action as the bustling tugs break the heavy ice.

SKIES

Skies are exciting to do in watercolor. One of the first things to learn is that a sky must be done rapidly with no second guessing. Once you have committed yourself, do not go back into it and try to change areas (unless you are working "wet-on-wet" and intend to mold some passages). I find the best way to learn to paint skies is to save "failures" and use the backsides of them to do quick sky studies—not with the intent of doing a painting, but merely to find how to achieve the feeling of what is going on in the sky.

Frequently the sky has beautiful, fluffy masses of cloud accentuated by an infinity of intensely blue background. To capture this, choose an exciting area and begin with a brushload of clear water. (You'll have to work fast because it will all change in three or four minutes.)

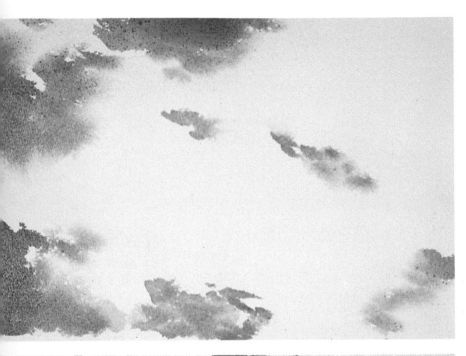

Step One. Working on a dry sheet, generously wet the edges and shadow areas of the clouds. Load a large brush with ultramarine to which a small amount of cerulean has been added and dash in the largest areas of blue, working up to the moist cloud edges so that a soft edge results. Occasionally stay in dry areas so you can obtain small bits of hard, ragged edges as well. Then spot in a few blue "holes" in the cloud mass, keeping the edges soft.

Step Two. Now mix a slightly warm gray, using ultramarine and vermilion with just a touch of cadmium orange. Put in the deepest shadow areas of the clouds, starting at the lower soft, wet edges where the blue sky begins so that this will blend readily. It is important to match the moist areas with a similar degree of moisture in your brush as you do this. Too moist a shadow wash will fan out into the blue, while too dry a brush will pick up blue, which will result in a hard edge or spottiness as it dries. As you work up into the cloud areas, dilute your gray with more water and occasionally brush into the dry area with a light touch to obtain some dry brush edges of very pale shadow value. Important: now leave it alone and settle for what you have.

This procedure can also be reversed by painting the clouds first, then adding the blue sky last. The difficulty here is that it is easy to spend too long on the clouds so that the edges may start to dry before you can apply the blue.

MORNING AND EVENING SKIES

Step One. This second approach works well for a morning or evening sky. In the first stage a thin, wet wash of cadmium orange was laid over the entire area, deepening it toward the horizon with more orange. The largest cloud in the upper right was put into the moist sky with a slightly purple wash (ultramarine with a bit more vermilion than for a neutral gray).

Step Two. This was also touched into the wash along the horizon to suggest distant cloud cover or haze. The sky was then allowed to dry completely.

The above-mentioned cloud wash was used again, but first the dry sky was misted with clean water from the spray bottle and allowed to stand until the shine disappeared from the surface. The cloud masses were laid in, starting at the top and working down. The middle area happened to be a little drier, which was fortunate, since the long strings of clouds in that particular area came out practically dry brush, giving more definition and a change of pace. The area below them was still moist enough for those clouds to spread more, giving softness to the distance. With care, a hairdryer can be used to control drying in desired areas—this chanced to be accidental.

A little warmer wash (orange added) formed a blur for the tree tops. Brush-handling gave them character. Finally, the foreground, skyline, and trees were completed.

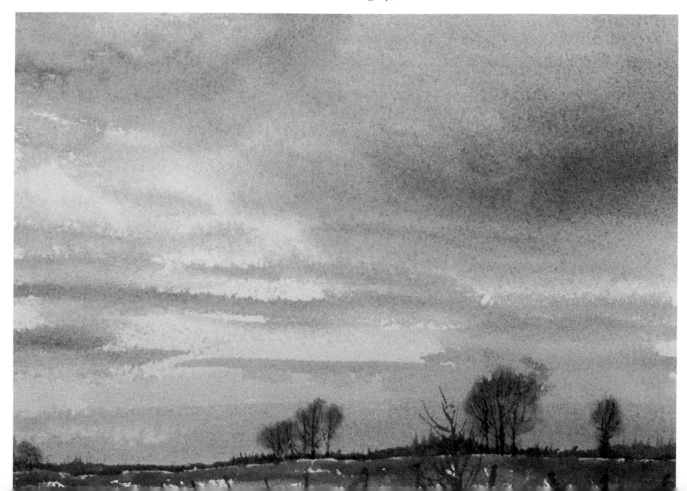

CLOUD LAYERS

Step One. The use of large clouds at the zenith and successively thinner layers of cloud suggest distance, while creating restful horizontals for a peaceful farm landscape. The blue was painted with a large brush and a load of color—ultramarine with a bit of vermilion at the top, then pure ultramarine. Lower down, cerulean was added to the ultramarine, then cerulean was used alone, and finally cerulean with a touch of cadmium yellow pale to give a greenish cast near the horizon. Some of the edges were softened with a damp, clean brush.

Step Two. The lower surfaces of the clouds received a wash of gray, deepening toward the bottom. Some edges were soft, some drybrushed—so that soft, hard, and drybrush or rough edges existed together, giving variety. Lastly a simple fall landscape was painted on the horizon.

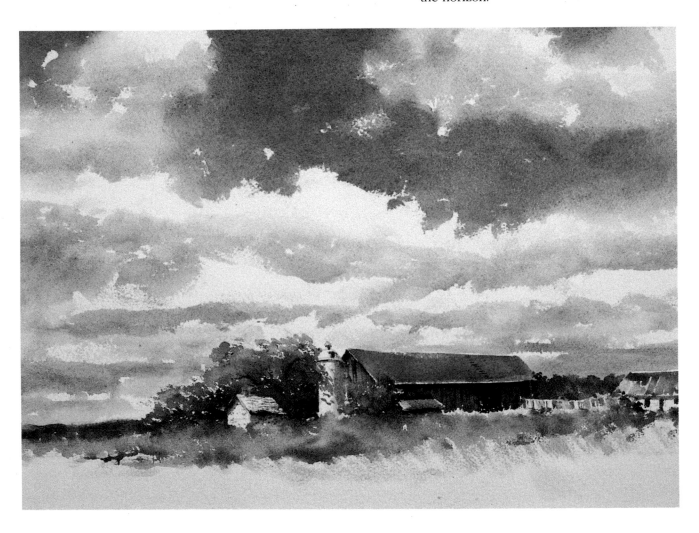

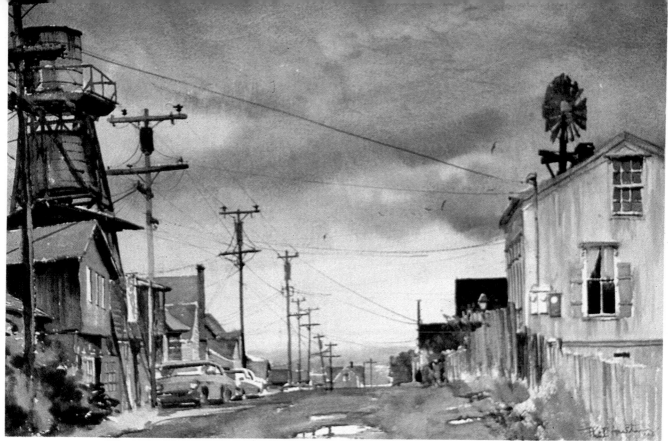

The stormy sky is clearing here, telling the story of lifting weather. The complex pattern of surrounding poles, water tanks, windmill, and buildings is held to a series of relatively simple contrasts, the darkest spot being roof silhouettes against the dark sky.

Rainy Alley, Mendocino
14½ × 21½ inches
Collection of Dr. and Mrs.
Paul Swade

STORMY SKY

Step One. In this stormy sky the first wash was applied very wet so that considerable molding of values could be done. The extremely light areas were avoided, then moistened with clear water, blending all edges. In the upper sky a mixture of mostly ultramarine and cerulean with just a small amount of vermilion was used. In the lower sky, cerulean with a small bit of cadmium yellow pale was used.

Step Two. At this point either of two methods is a possibility. You can go into the wet wash with a brushload of a rich mixture of ultramarine and vermilion, and form the tumbling clouds and the drippy ones just above the light horizontal. Or, if you prefer better control, allow the first step to dry completely. Then mold the clouds, do the lower ribbons of dark, and gently mist the entire sky with a little clear water so that soft blending occurs. When all is dry, the little farm scene below can be put in to complete the mood.

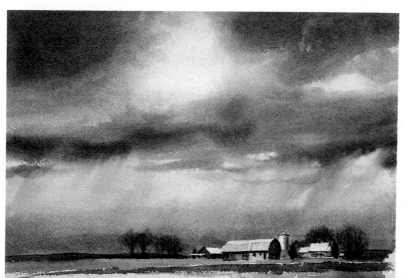

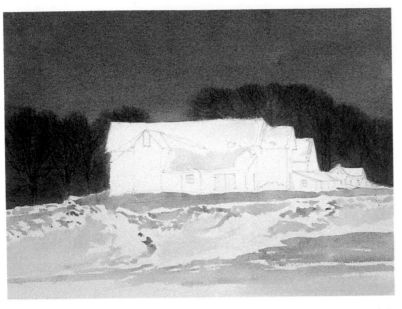

WINTER SKY

Step One. In the final sky demonstration a mixture of ultramarine, cerulean, and vermilion created a cold winter sky. A flat wash was laid down, carefully painting around the building area with its snowy roofs. A small amount of alizarin was laid into the damp wash near the horizon. While the wash was very damp, cadmium orange was also dropped in for the color of tree limbs and branches in late night. Then the surface was lightly marred with a slender brush-handle to indicate the tree forms in detail. As the washes dried, brush-handle work on the main trunks and limbs left a light line, indicating light falling on these areas. Some portions of bare roof were indicated as well as snow shadows.

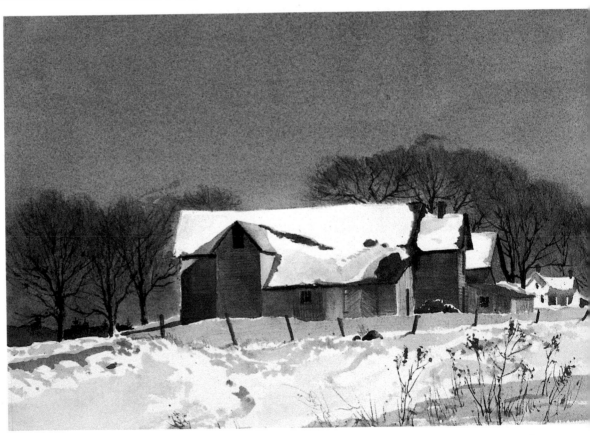

Step Two. In this second step a dark horizon was added on the left and the buildings were completed, as were the snow shadows, fence posts, and weeds in the foreground.

SNOWFALL

Step One. A snow scene is depicted first. It was painted in a strong value to allow for the brightening that occurred when the snowflakes were put in. Liquid mask was used to hold the whites of the birches.

The largest area, the dark stormy sky, was laid in and the shapes of the birch trees were added into the damp sky with a mixture of alizarin, vermilion, and a little ultramarine. Then brush-handle work suggested many of the limbs. The evergreen skyline was added while some dampness remained in the sky wash. When this was completely dry the masking was removed. Small detail and some additional values in the snow emphasized the large simple whites. Next all the detail was finished in the trees, building, and foreground.

Step Two. A discarded Dexter no. 3 mat blade with its long point was used to pick out the snowflakes. It is a rather tedious chore, but it makes the snowfall convincing because snowflakes can be varied in size with complete control, to give the painting depth. Also, because of the control any type of snowfall, flurries, occasional flakes, or a heavy fall can be indicated.

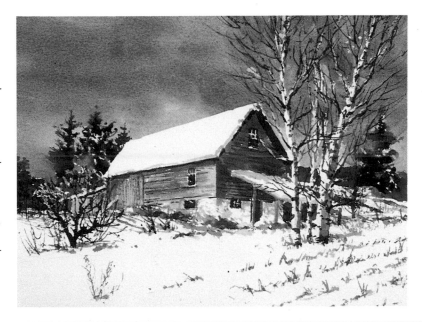

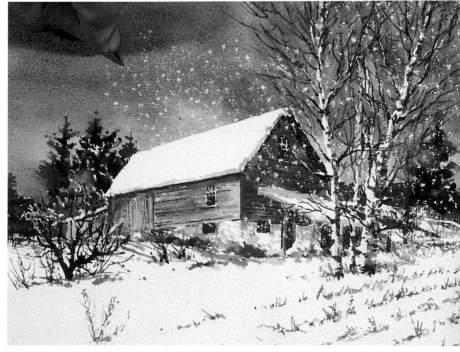

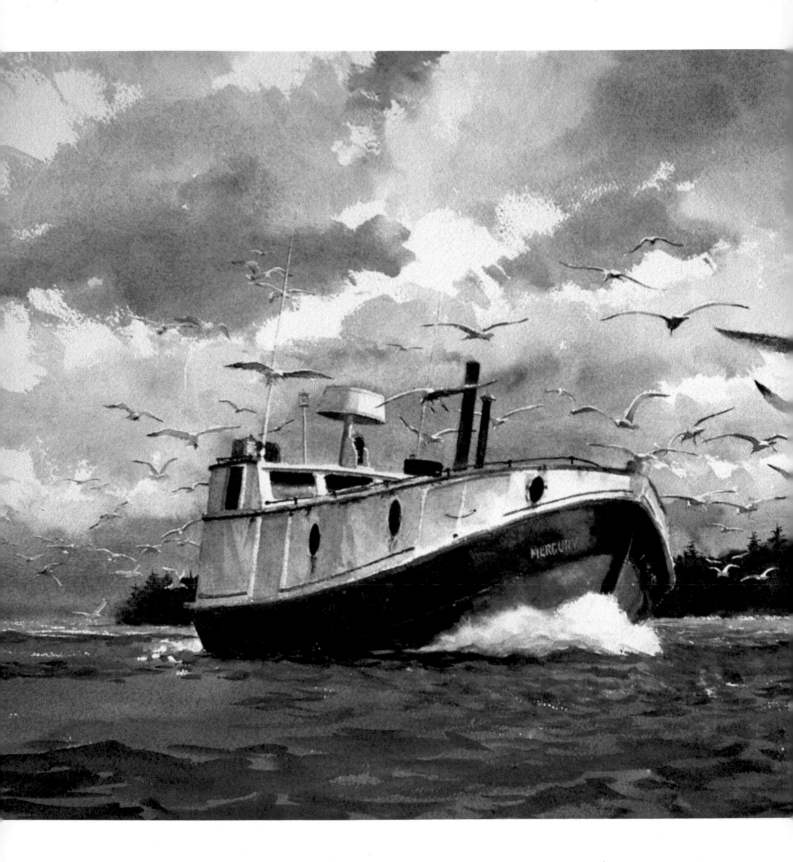

8. Step-by-Step Demonstrations

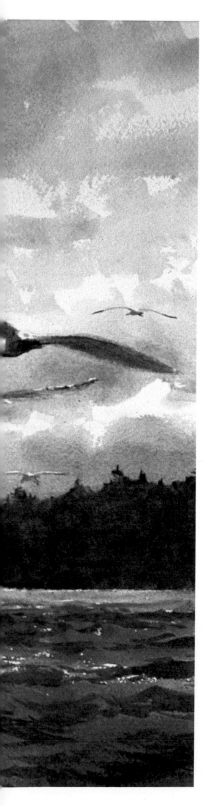

In this series of demonstrations I will present a variety of subject material to show that any season can be depicted using combinations of the colors in a limited palette. The compositions are widely varied to demonstrate different procedures. Planning varies for each, dictated by the subject material itself. Studying these paintings step by step along with those shown earlier in the book and those contained in the portfolio which follows these five demonstrations should be of help.

When a fishing boat is escorted by a lot of gulls, it usually means a good catch since it indicates the crew is still cleaning the catch. I used liquid masking to hold white areas for the gulls and details of the boat, and this gave me the freedom to do the sky rapidly.

Returning Gillnetter
21 × 29 inches
Collection of Mr. and Mrs.
Lee Wendell

95

THE SUMMER SKY

This old farm stands out with a sweep of distance surrounding it. It always creates an interesting pattern against whatever kind of sky exists on that particular day.

Step One. I made several exploratory thumbnail sketches, varying the size and number of buildings and experimenting with different horizon levels. I then decided on a sky of large fluffy clouds since the sky would cover a large area of the painting.

After the buildings and trees were drawn lightly on a sheet of 300-pound Arches paper, I sponged the sheet heavily with clean water

and allowed it to soak for several minutes. Then I used a rolled-up towel to remove the surface moisture. I then again applied clean water to the areas where cloud edges would appear.

A mixture of ultramarine and cerulean was flowed in rapidly and very wet with a small amount of vermilion added at the very top of the sheet. Clean water was again used to soften some edges where the flow had not been adequate. The important thing here is to get a pleasing mixture of hard, soft, and irregular edges. Larger clouds were formed high up in the sky, diminishing in size toward the horizon to give perspective.

Step Two. Now I used a mixture of vermilion, ultramarine, and just a touch of orange to create the color for cloud shadows. This was washed in rapidly, constantly using another brush of clean water to keep the upper reaches of the shadows very soft. As before, I maintained a mixture of soft, hard, and irregular edges. I indicated a few tiny holes in some cloud areas by dropping in a touch of the blue sky color—wet. Care must be taken at this stage to make sure the sky color doesn't run over areas where it might influence color or value later.

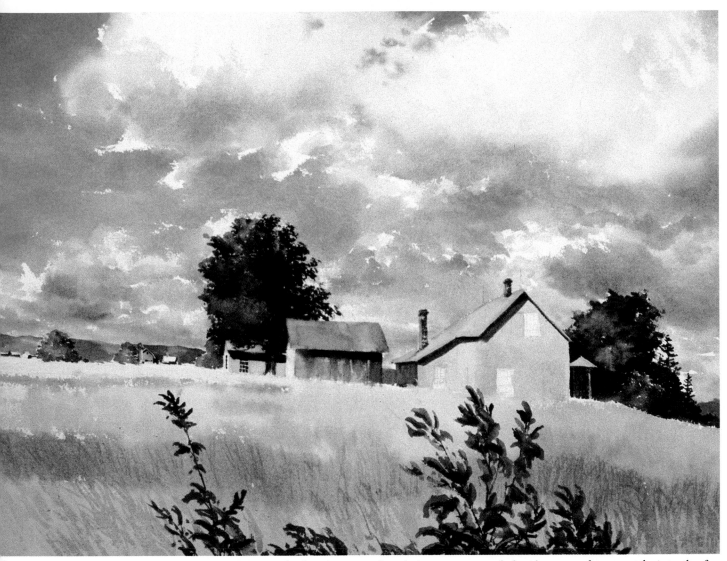

Step Three. With the sky completed, it was now possible to key the sunlit areas to create a proper relationship of values. The large foreground band was now done very wet, allowing the opportunity to blend in subtle value and color changes with a light accent near the buildings. I used the brush handle to indicate detail in the greener areas. This must be done very lightly and gently, bruising the paper just enough for deeper color to settle into the furrows created.

The basic values were laid in on the buildings, allowing for lost and found edges. The trees were then put in, molded by the three-step process discussed in Chapter 6. Now the subdued cooler greens were laid in along the horizon. There were now no blank areas in the painting and values had been well adjusted, but little detail had been added.

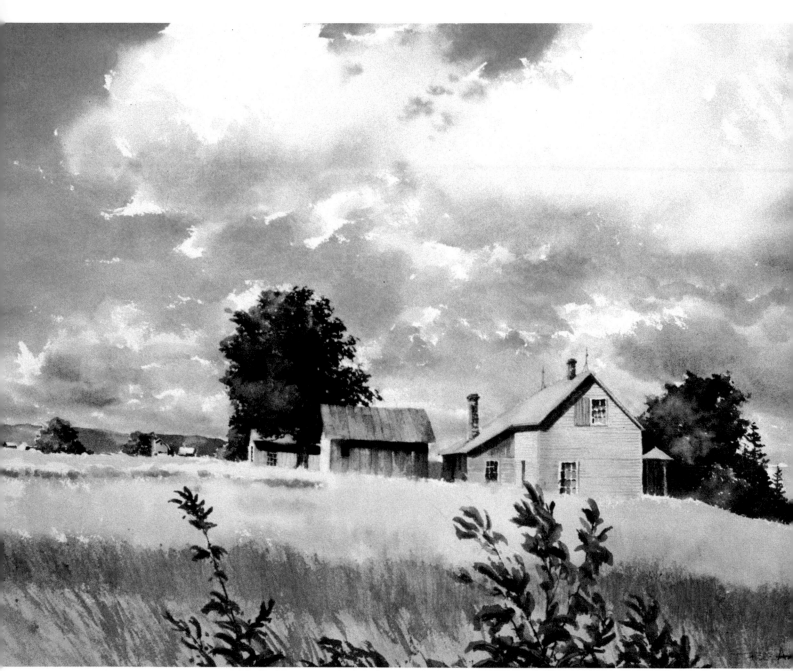

The Summer Sky
21½ × 29 inches

Step Four. Detail was added now, beginning with the principal center of interest, the house. Less and less detail was needed toward the further reaches of the landscape. Finally I added the swaying brush in the foreground, working progressively from light to medium and dark values. A few last-minute accents were added, a deeper shadow here and there, an additional change of value or color on buildings, and the painting was finished.

SWEEPING IN, MENDOCINO

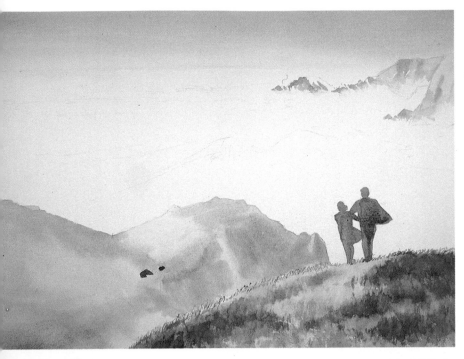

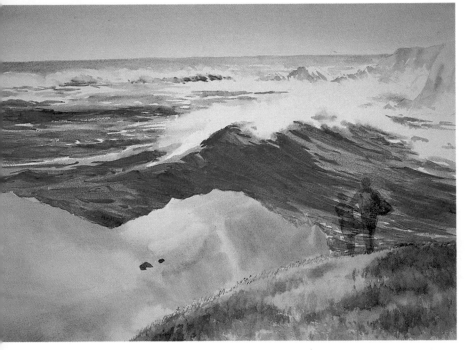

Step One. The paper, a sheet of 300-pound Arches cold press, was washed off with a sponge and water and allowed to dry before the drawing was done. This makes a better working surface and must be done before penciling since washing sets the pencil lines, making it impossible to erase them. Liquid mask was applied to figures, holes through the rocks, and the grass fringe. This allows freedom in doing large washes. A light sky with even more light at the horizon was flowed on. A predominantly orange wash (a little ultramarine and vermilion added) was carried over the large foreground rock mass with some variation in value. Then the foreground was covered with a similar wash, and darker value and texture added for the grass. Brush handle work and directional strokes of dry brush helped with the texture.

The lower edges of the distant shore and offshore rocks were moistened with water. Then the light color for the rocks and shore was painted down to this moist edge, giving the soft edge of spray. Slightly darker values for contour were added as the light wash was drying.

Step Two. The edge of spray and distant rolling waves were moistened with clean water before starting the sweeping wash for the ocean. The light areas were a mixture of cerulean and viridian, the dark areas a mixture of ultramarine and viridian. Brush strokes all followed the flow of the water. This color was brought up to the premoistened edges for softness. A lighter value of the cerulean was laid into the moist areas within the white spray for soft passages of motion. Curling brush strokes gave roll to the distant wave. The horizon was washed with a lighter value of cerulean and painted down to the moist top of the wave. Deepest values of the sea water were added while the surface was still slightly damp so there would be no hard edges.

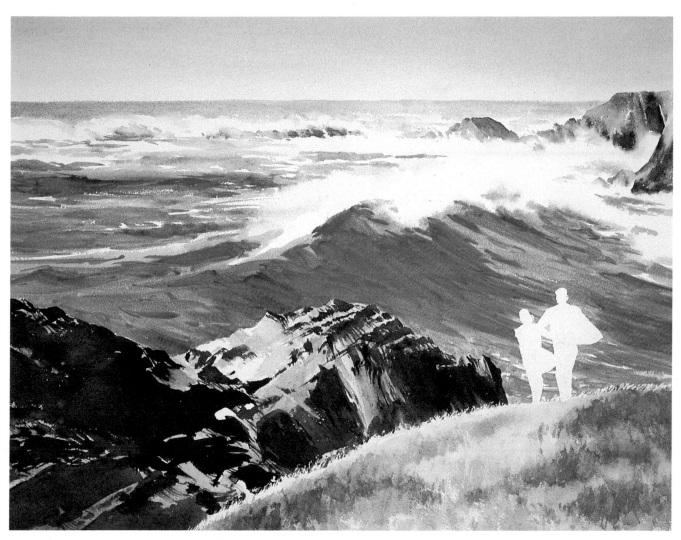

Step Three. The darker areas of the mass of foreground rock were now painted with a wash of ultramarine, vermilion, and a little cadmium orange for warmth. Changes in value, as well as a small degree of change in color, added interest and character. More light and more change were introduced near the figures but simplified, with larger passages of dark toward the left. Similar color, but lighter value, was used for the distant coast. Finally, the liquid mask was removed.

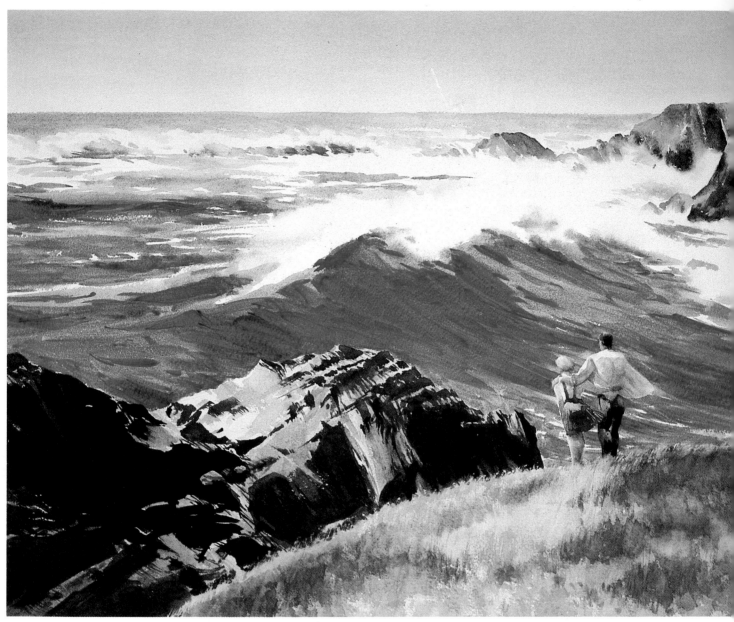

Sweeping In, Mendocino
21½ × 28½ inches

Step Four. The color of the sea was added to the small holes in the rocks. The figures were completed with a loose treatment to match the rest of the painting. The grassy fringe of the hill was completed and the painting studied for any finishing details. A damp brush was used to soften the edges of the figures here and there to keep them from looking like cutouts.

I originally painted this scene on the Mendocino coast (sans figures), inadvertently getting drenched in the process. The original was destroyed in a fire, but fortunately I had a number of good slides of the coast and the surf, and even a slide of the original painting. I decided to try it again, adding figures to give scale and help suggest the windy day.

UP ON SUGAR HILL

This little hillside meadow surrounded by woods and some old fieldstone walls has always had a special charm, particularly in the fall when the distant blue ridge sets off the brilliance of the maples. After making several thumbnail sketches, I decided to add an old sugar shed and name it "Sugar Hill," thereby giving the painting a further dimension. The nearby overhead branches were added, since they seemed to increase the intimacy of the spot.

Step One. To give the flooding warmth of fall, a thin wash of cadmium orange, slightly grayed, was laid over all of the field grass. The bright yellow and orange was splashed in for the mass of trees on the right. Working rapidly with lots of moist color, I washed in the ridge with a mixture of ultramarine, cerulean, and a trace of vermilion. Into this wet surface splashes of cadmium orange, yellow, and vermilion were added at the lower edge, blending the fall color into the distance. The sky also was quickly added, allowing a soft blend along the top of the ridge, avoiding the limbs, and tucking it in around the colorful trees on the right. A trace of cadmium orange in the wash gave warmth above the ridge while more blue in the upper right suggested distant sky, as well as contrasting with the bright trees. Texture was added to the grassy field, bright leaves were added on and along the wall, and a simple gray wash was painted on the rocks, leaving adequate white paper.

Step Two. More color was added to the group of trees on the right. A little gray partially eliminated some of the white left for the shed. Darks were added for the distant wall. The overhead limbs received a varied gray wash as did the fenceposts. The nearby fenceposts were darkened as well as parts of the overhead limbs so that the strongest darks were now in the foreground. While the sky was still damp some vermilion with cadmium orange and ultramarine was blurred into the sky above the trees on the right to make a warm brown while a cooler wash was blurred in for tree forms along the ridge to the left.

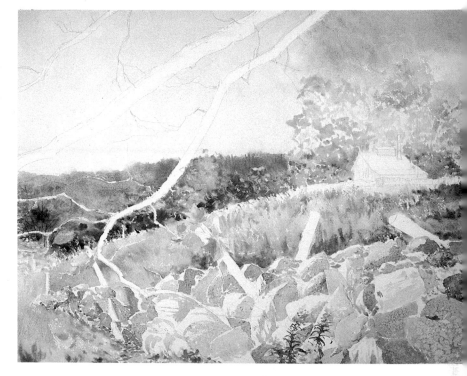

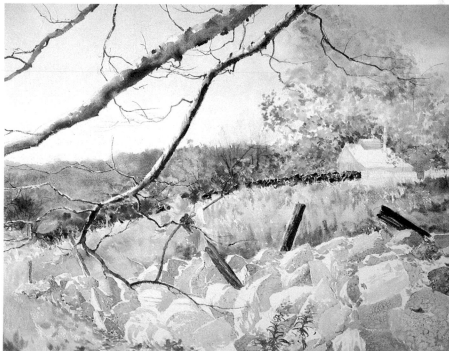

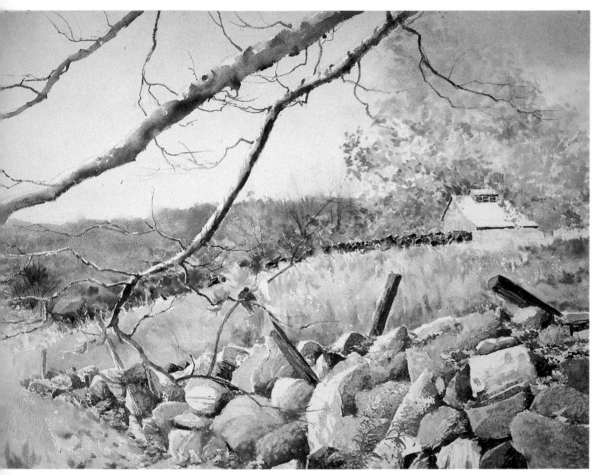

Step Three. A varying wash, cool and warm, was added to the rocks of the wall. Once a gray is mixed with ultramarine and vermilion on your palette, it is easy in painting a wall like this to add a bit more orange with one brushful, a bit more blue with the next, or a bit more vermilion, so that your color and value keep changing slightly from stone to stone. A few rocks were left pure white or nearly so. Table salt was sprinkled into the wall; it gathers the pigment (if it is very moist) in little blotches and creates a nice stone texture. Finally, deep values and shadow were added to the wall. The woodpile by the sugar shed got a brown wash and detail was added to parts of the shed.

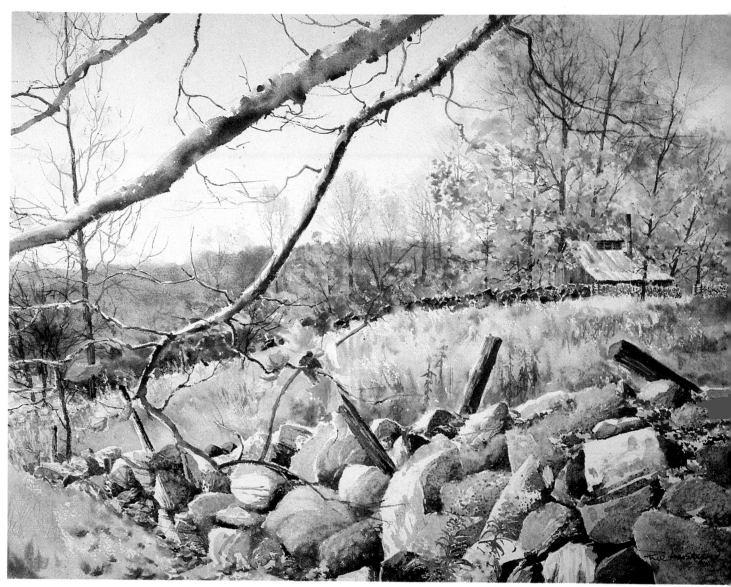

Up on Sugar Hill
21½ × 28½ inches

Step Four. Final color and shape were added to leaves on the overhead limb and the leaves on and along the wall. Detail was added to the woodpile, and I decided to make the sugar shed red with leaves partially obscuring it. Tree trunks were woven into the trees around the shed and along the distant wall. Saplings were put in at the left by the end of the rock pile, and a tall tree was added behind the overhead limbs to break up their outward motion and tie the left side of the painting together. Limbs and branches were added where need-

ed. The sugar shed received a metal roof of blue-gray with vermilion rust spots.

While doing the painting I have frequently tested it with a mat closing out all side distractions to study it carefully. In the end, the important thing is to stop before overworking any part of it. Some weeds were placed in the middle ground. A little more bright color was splashed into the foliage on the right to loosen it up a bit, and the painting was ready for the signature.

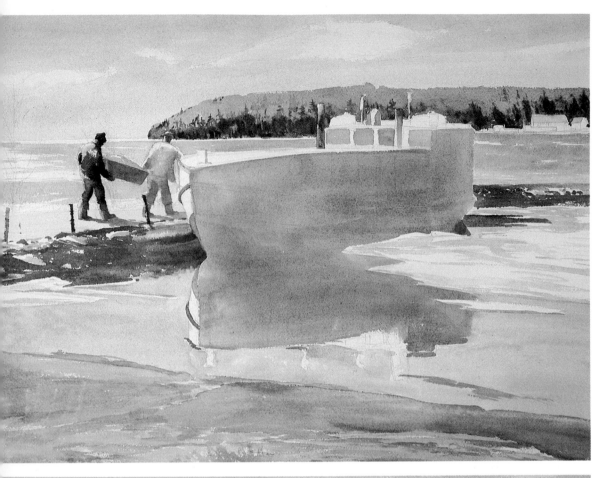

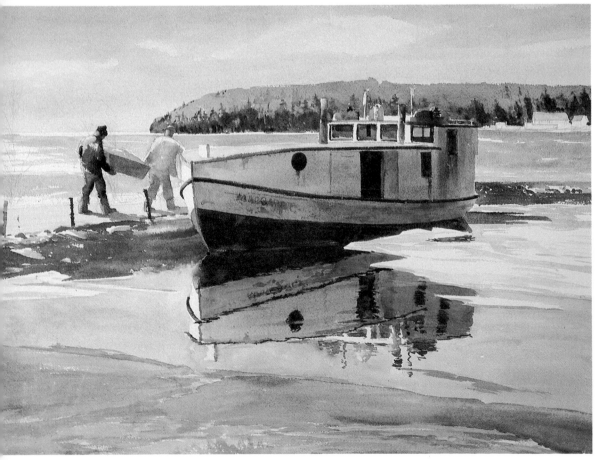

OPENING UP

Wooden gillnetters, used by commercial fishermen to harvest whitefish, are gradually being replaced by newer steel models. The old wood hulls have a special charm, though some scornfully refer to them as "old shoe boxes." In the spring the fishermen eagerly await the breakup of the ice so they can get out of the harbors and start setting nets.

Step One. I decided to suggest this eagerness by having men carrying a box of nets out to prepare the "Margaret," as she sat among the last of the harbor ice, with the drifting ice beyond. Having carefully planned and penciled my design on a sheet of 300-pound Arches cold press, I began to work rapidly on a dry sheet with a large brush loaded with color, to create a big pattern. Floating clouds in a pale sky of cerulean and cadmium yellow pale came first, then ultramarine for the distant water with the white of the paper for floating ice. The large triangle of quiet water came next, then the entire shadow side of the boat and the reflection—one gradually deepening value, washed in with a mixture of ultramarine, cerulean, and a bit of vermilion. A light and dark figure was blocked in, a warm dark suggested the dock, a wash of cadmium orange with a bit of ultramarine and vermilion represented the wet sand in the foreground, and a gray dominated by orange created the far shore. A mixture of ultramarine and vermilion made the value to which viridian was added for the deep green trees along the far shoreline. This blurs slightly into the warm gray, giving distance.

Step Two. The shadow side of the boat was deepened toward the lower part of the hull and toward the rear, forcing the front end forward. Values were also deepened considerably in the reflection. While this was still damp, scrubbed and chipped paint was indicated and the name "Margaret" was added. The lower hull received a wash of dark green (prepared as for the evergreens mentioned above). Spots of dark gave accent to portholes, open doors, and windows of the pilot house. Smokestacks and running lights were added. Reminder: from the pilot's viewpoint the red is on his left and the green on his right!

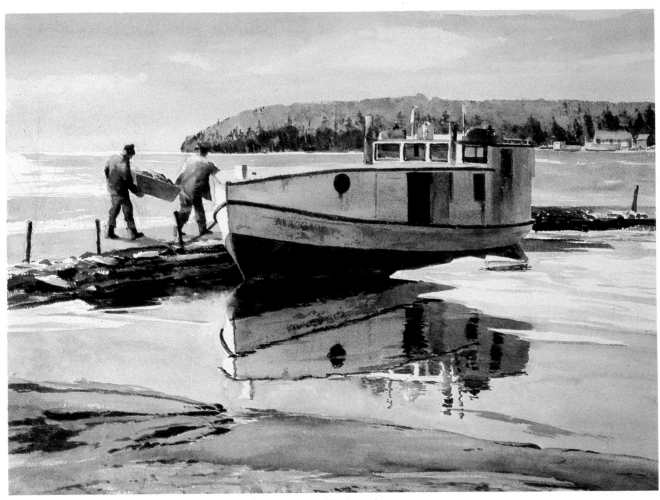

Step Three. Deep values were added to the dock, suggesting more detail. The figures were darkened in value. The distant dock, fish sheds, and boats seemed to need slightly more detail. The old posts along the dock were strengthened and at this point I decided there should be one behind the boat, closer to the margin than to the boat. A dark brown (a mixture of ultramarine, vermilion, and cadmium orange) was now used to put in shadows for rivulets on the shore, wet edges to the sand, and similar details. The same color was used for a hawser to tie the boat—about time! A lighter wash of the same color gave a little more shape to the sand.

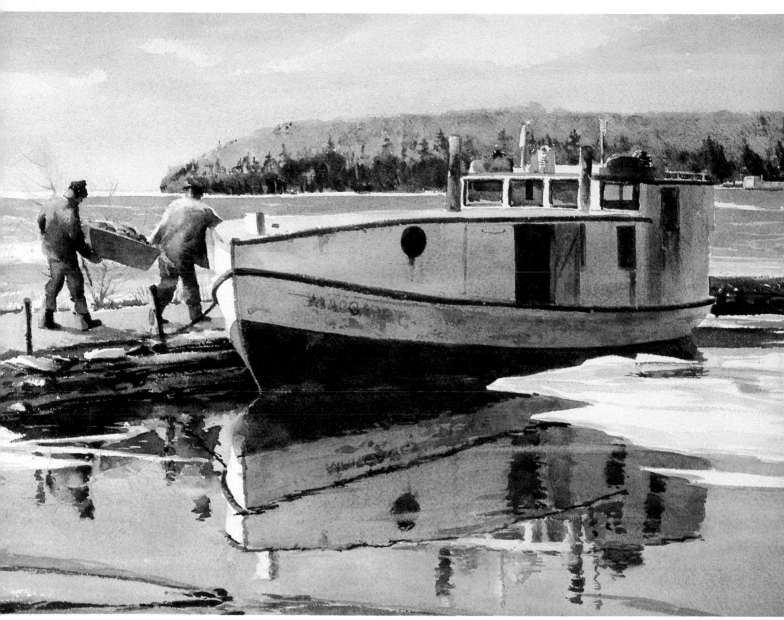

Opening Up
21½ × 18½ inches

Step Four. Studying the wedge of open water beneath the boat, I noticed this area needed to be a little deeper in value as well as slightly warmer, so I mixed a thin wash with cerulean and a bit of cadmium yellow pale, and with a large brush ran a quick wash across all but the snowy ice and white reflections. The improvement was noticeable. Somehow it looked more mirror-like. Then yellow grass was added on the far side of the dock as well as some slender saplings, put in with a mixture of cadmium orange and a little vermilion and ultramarine. The ends of the branches were blurred with a damp brush. Reflections of the posts, saplings, and figures were added to the still water. The wedge of water and ice containing the reflections actually has become the focal point. Reflections frequently are an exact duplication of the object, but I prefer some distortion, some fracturing from ripples and a deepening of the value of the reflection.

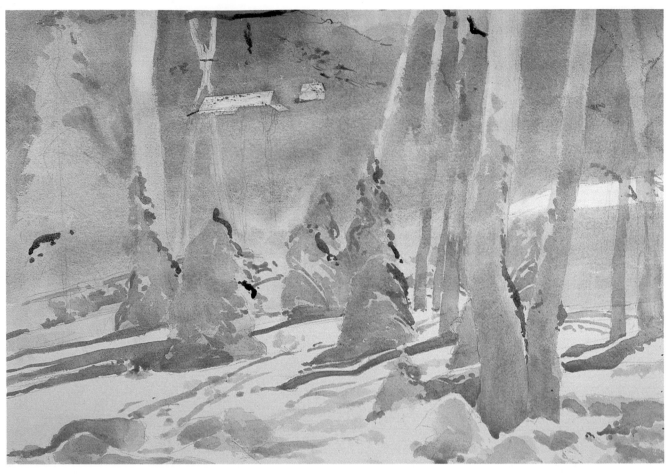

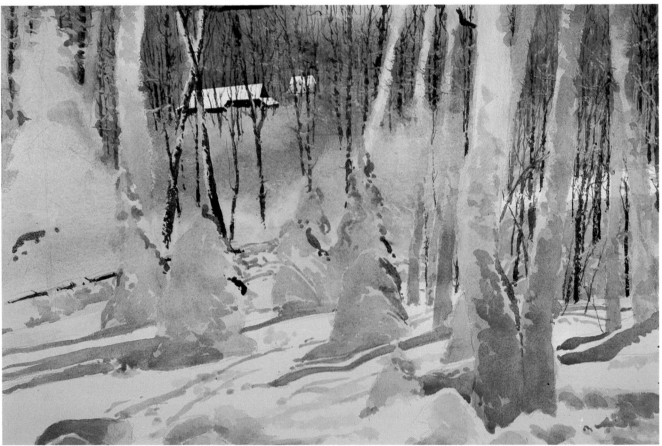

UP THROUGH THE WOODS

Step One. The scene was planned as usual through a process of several thumbnail sketches, with attention to having a large area almost pure white. It was then penciled lightly on a 22″ × 30″ sheet of 300-pound Arches rough paper. Liquid mask was applied to isolated whites contained in large areas of wash. Masking tape was used on a barn roof and a house back in the woods—an easy solution where simple angular forms are to be masked. The paper was now moistened by lightly passing over it with a wet sponge. Any traces of glisten were removed with the sponge. Then a wash of ultramarine and cerulean, with a small amount of vermilion to gray it slightly, was flowed freely over the upper area of the woods and all shadow areas of the snow on the ground and evergreens. The trunk areas were avoided and any excess bleeding of color into them was blotted up. (Use either a damp brush or a strip of soft blotter.) Darker variations in the wash were added adjacent to large, white areas, increasing contrast.

Step Two. More values were added in the large areas of blue wash, particularly the top quarter of the background, plus darker value on shadowed trunk areas, some mounds of snow in foreground, and some cast shadows. Branch forms were squeegeed out of the damp wash with a brush handle. A mix of ultramarine, vermilion, and cadmium orange (to produce a dark gray) was now used to indicate distant trees. The masking tape was removed from the building and the nearer trees were then painted in, together with a simple indication of the buildings.

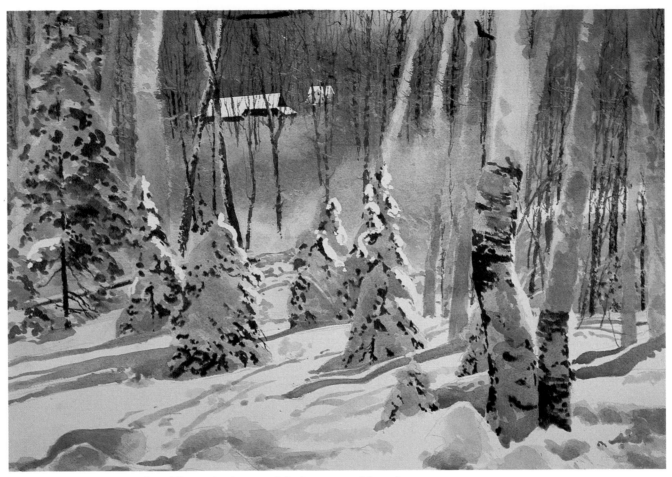

Step Three. A mixture of dark green, achieved by mixing ultramarine and vermilion, then adding enough viridian to make a green, was used on the evergreens, allowing branches to peek out from beneath masses of snow. A warm gray mixture of ultramarine, vermilion, and some cadmium orange was added to birch trunks where no snow was clinging. This change in color distinguished the light bark from the snow on the trunks. The liquid mask was removed from the evergreens, bringing out the whites of sunlight on snowy trees. Detail was given to the nearest trees. These were completed first since they carried the most detail. More distant trees carried less detail.

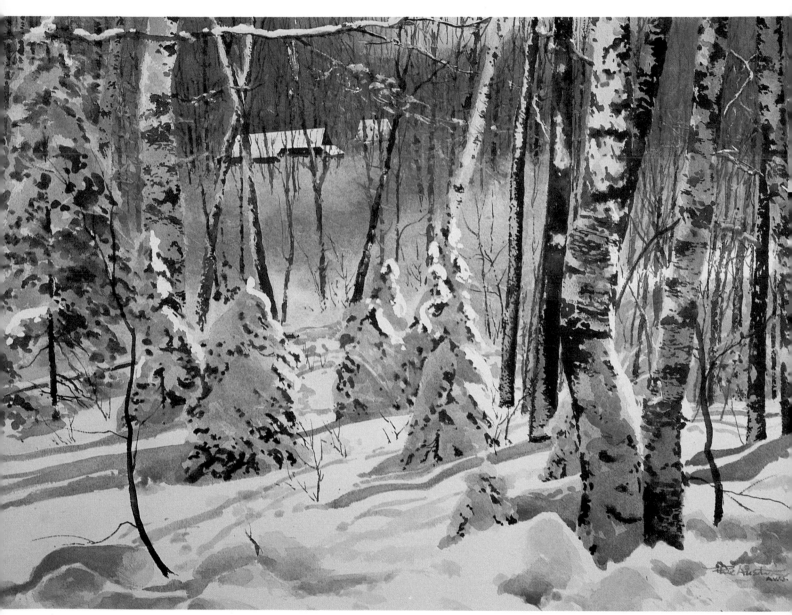

Step Four. The last of the liquid mask was removed, revealing snow-laden limbs of birches. Limb detail was added with dark gray, which was also used to place saplings in the foreground and twigs sticking up through the snow. A few slender trees were added in the background and a final decision was made to deepen the farthest woods with a wash of blue, grayed with vermilion and cadmium orange.

Up Through the Woods
21¹/₂ × 29 inches

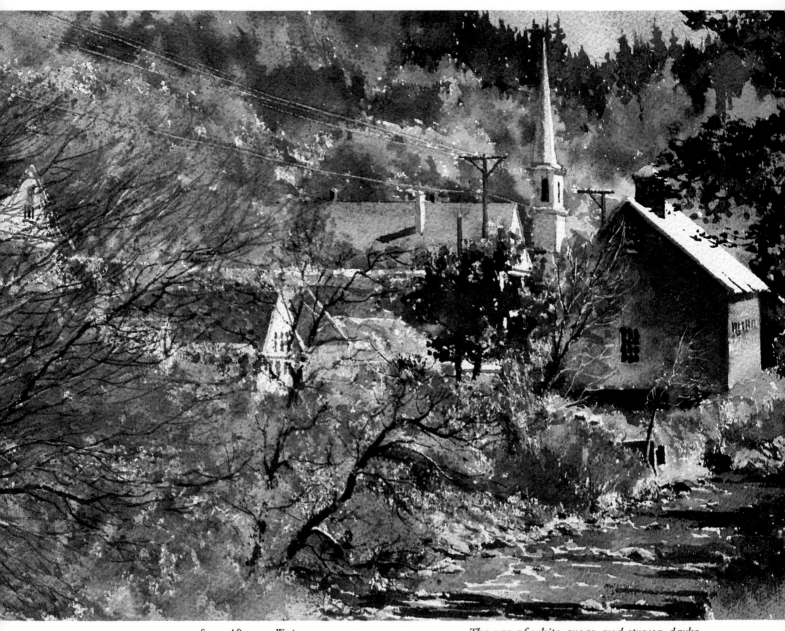

Sunny Afternoon, West Dover
11³/4 × 15⁵/8 inches

The use of white areas and strong darks was carefully planned to create contrast and draw the interest. Broken bits of warm yellows, orange, and olive greens created the screen of foliage, while cooler greens made the wooded ridge recede. The gradual changes in color created the sense of a quiet, peaceful village.

Depth was added by using sharp detail in the foreground branch work and breaking up the white areas slightly to push them back. Shadows created contour and flattened out the little brook.

Portfolio of Paintings

I am frequently asked, "How do you decide what you are going to paint?" or "Why are you doing a painting of that?"

Sometimes this is a hard question to answer. My reason for doing a painting has a great deal to do with how I feel about the way a field lies across a hilltop and disappears around a woodlot, about the sturdiness of an old log cabin standing alone against the woods, or a hundred-year-old stump, gray with age and rusty with decay. It may be scattered Queen Anne's Lace and Tyrolean Knapweed surrounding it that moves me to paint or the way fresh snow has drifted against a weathered, sagging building. In other words, I have a gut feeling that I'm looking at a good subject.

Teaching workshops has made me aware of the value in students learning not only the ways in which other artists work, but to see specific things demonstrated such as the painting of water, reflections, cloudy skies, foregrounds, trees—in short to watch a painting in progress from start to finish. It is also helpful to review a variety of paintings together with comments regarding the choice of subject, ideas employed, and procedure. That is the reason for the following pages, a portfolio of paintings accompanied by such captions.

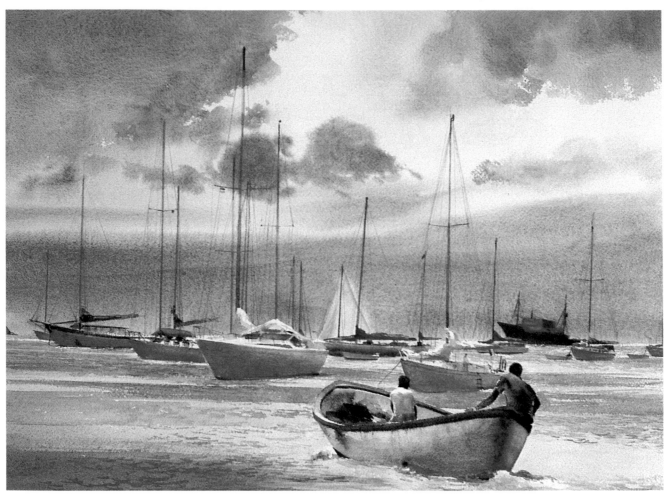

Harbor Boys, Sint Maarten
21 × 29 inches
Collection of Mr. and Mrs.
Frank Mohr

In this painting, the sky is primarily the center of interest with exciting clouds, a good deal of texture, changing values, and a lot of action. Being able to get a continuous variation of grays with the limited palette was also important to this work. It was painted in the studio from a series of slides taken in the West Indies. The rain was moving in when I got the interesting sky. Several slides provided the information needed to paint the yachts riding at anchor, while a shot with a zoom lens provided the necessary detail for the boys in the double ender.

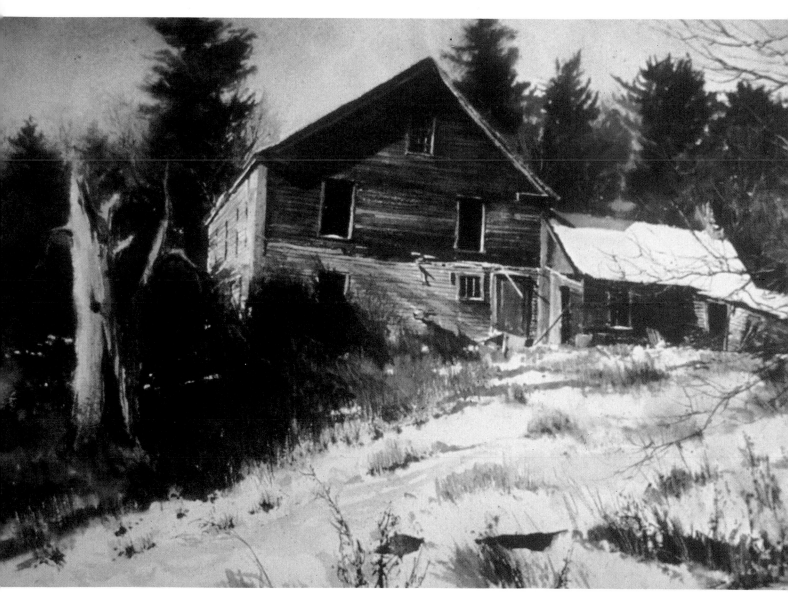

This old house stands on Catamount
Mountain in New Hampshire. The lights and
darks, as well as the placement of the trees,
were adjusted to emphasize the dilapidated
building. The old, shattered stump was
invented as a partner in the collapse.

Collapsing Dream
21¹/₂ × 29¹/₂ inches
Collection of Elmer Fox & Co.

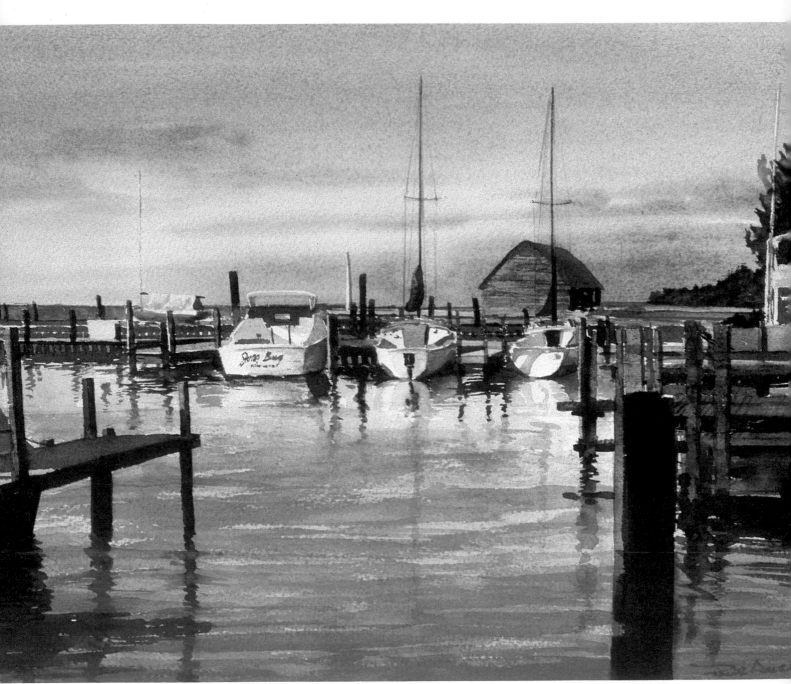

Here the late light and sweeping horizontals create a cool, peaceful atmosphere. The dark shapes flanking a central negative space emphasize the boats at their moorings.

Evening, Ephraim Harbor
11½ × 15⅝ inches

118

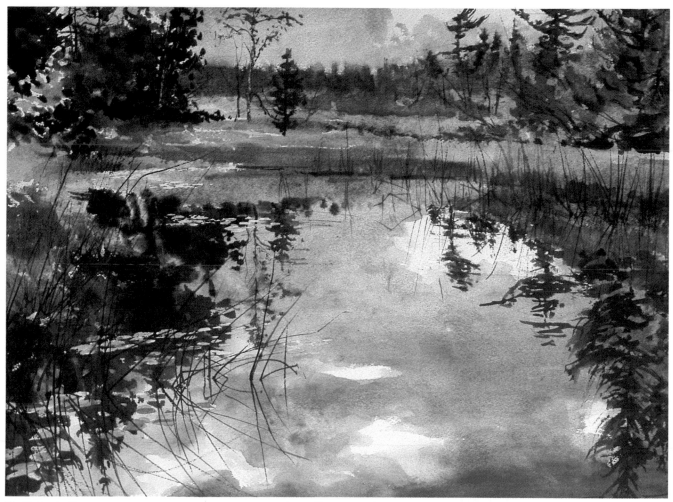

The Big Swale, The Ridges
Sanctuary
$11^1/_2 \times 15^5/_8$ *inches*

The reflections of trees, reeds, and clouds form the major point of interest in this painting. The water, grass, and sky were all worked very moist. The details were added when the painting was about dry.

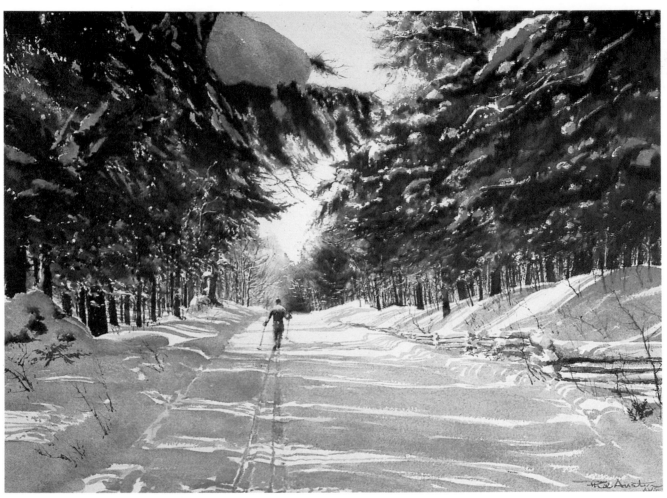

To capture the feeling of solitude and calm
that is part of the morning after a new
snowfall, I began by applying liquid mask
to hold areas of white for snow on the
branches. I then washed in the sky and all
the green mass of trees. The snow shadows
were a mixture of cerulean and a little
alizarin, applied rapidly and very wet. A bit
of mist from the spray bottle when they were
complete caused the alizarin to float
slightly, giving a pink glow to the landscape.

First Track
21½ × 29 inches
Collection of Kearney and
Trecker Corp.

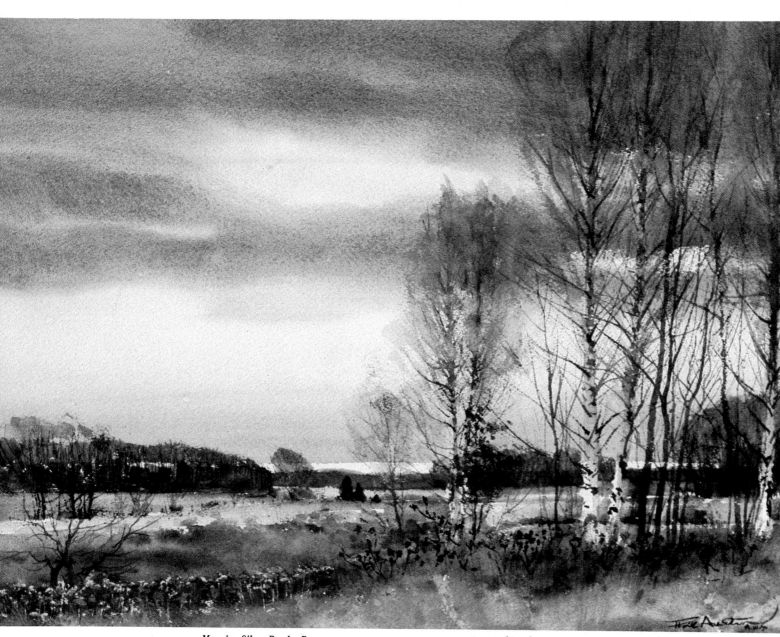

Morning Silver, Rowley Bay
$11^{1}/_{2} \times 15^{5}/_{8}$ *inches*

For a brief moment as I painted, the sun came through a rift in the clouds and turned the distant water to shining silver. It gave life to the soft grays and browns of fall.

The challenge here was to get the gradual cooling of color from foreground up into the distant hills. A thin wash of cadmium orange created the tawny grass.

Down into a California Valley
$15^5/_8 \times 11^1/_2$ inches

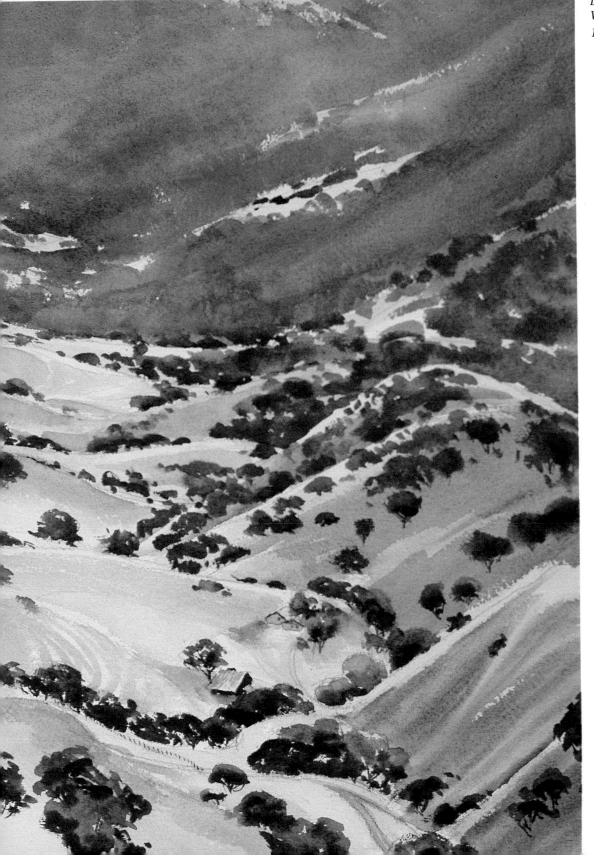

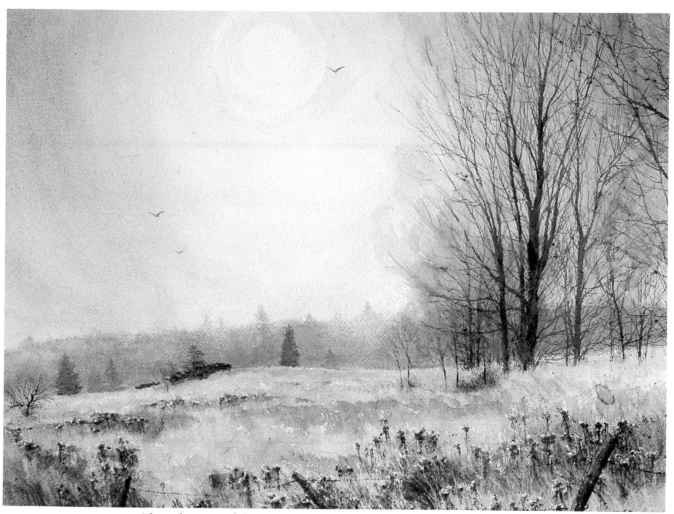

The soft areas of this painting were completed working wet-on-wet on 300-pound Arches paper. After those areas were completed, I used dry-brush and brush-handle techniques to create texture in the foreground. Masking was used to hold light areas for weed heads. The trees, fence, hawks, and final details on weeds were added to the dry surface.

Indian Summer
21 × 29 inches

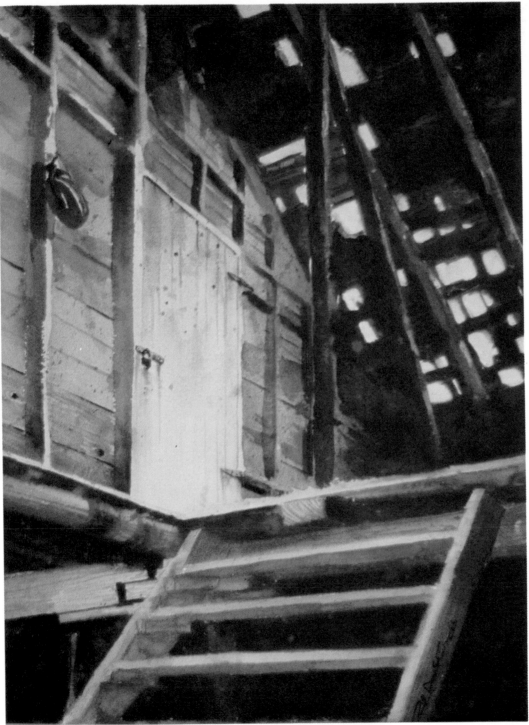

Loft with Skylight
15⅝ × 11½ inches

This old loft was bathed with light because of a lot of missing shingles in the roof. A gray-green wash for the lighter areas gives an eerie look. The geometric patterns are beautiful.

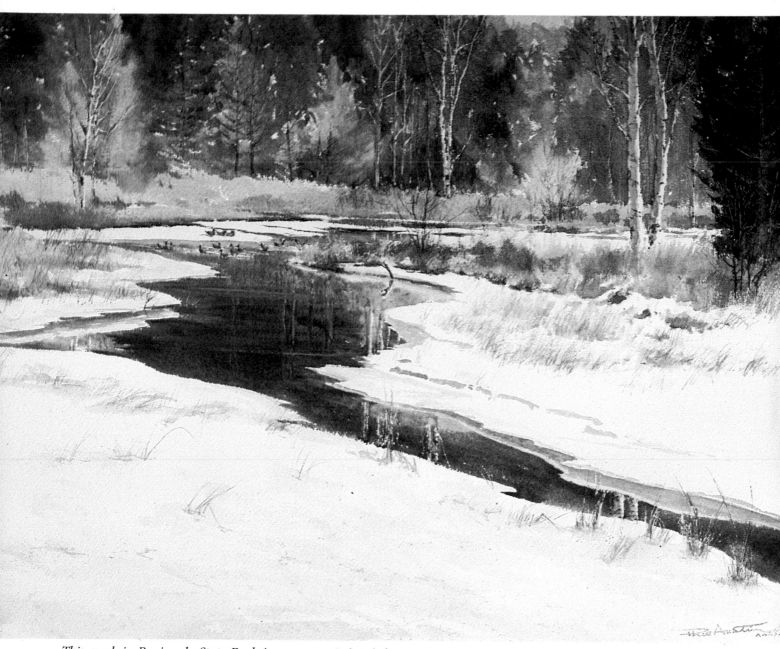

This creek in Peninsula State Park is a
winter treat. It is always different. The ice
never opens up with the same pattern twice.
The woods catch the light differently at
different times, and the pattern of weed
stalks and dry grass varies with the depth of
the snow. In this case, ducks had also
moved in, adding activity. The white snow
creates excellent negative space against the
dark water.

Early Arrivals
21 × 29 inches
Collection of Kearney and
Trecker Corp.

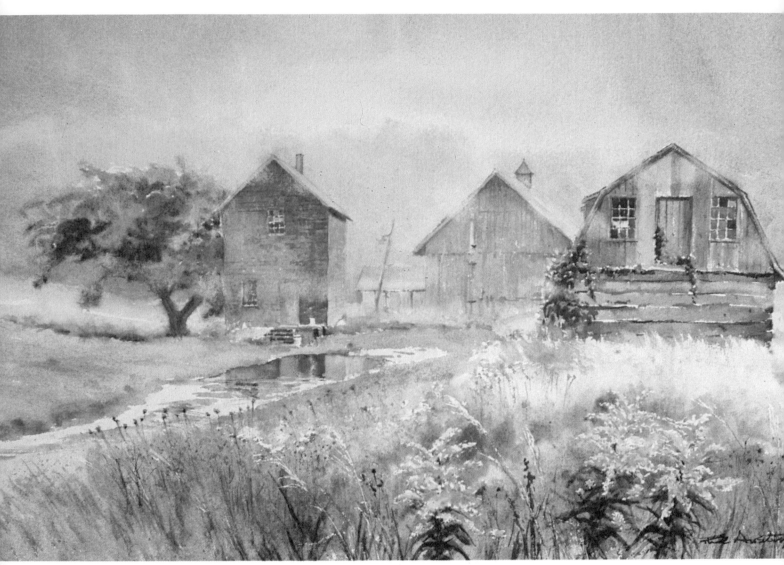

This on-location painting was exciting to do because of the subtly modulating colors. I worked very wet, first using liquid mask to hold white for the goldenrod, some grasses, and weeds. After this dried, I removed the mask and added fresh yellow, then misted it gently with a spray bottle. After a minute or two, I dragged a few ribbons of fog across the buildings by picking up a little of the softened wash here and there.

Fall Fog
14 1/4 × 21 1/2 inches

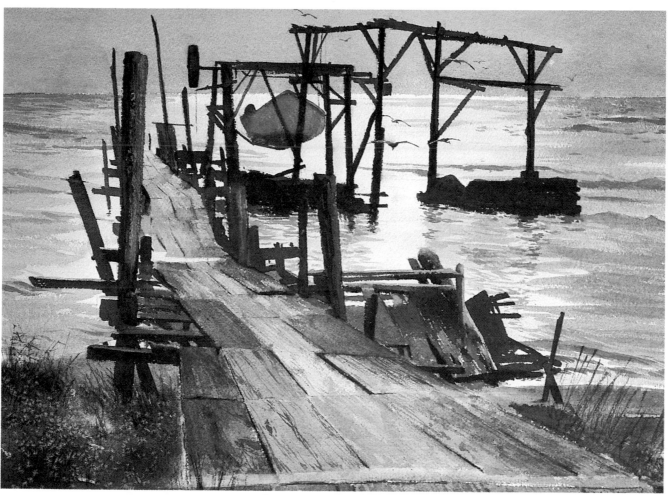

Morning Boat Sling at Jacksonport

21¹/₂ × 29¹/₂ inches
Collection of Kearney and Trecker Corp.

Light and dark areas are extremely important in this painting. They set the mood and create the pattern. The light dock leads in, but is contained on the left by the dark piling and horizontal support timbers. The blue boat silhouette carries the eye into the maze of angular supports. The dark cribs below give these supports a solid base, and the dark mass at the water's edge brings the eye back to the starting place. The graceful gulls in flight help make the white glare of light on the water more interesting.

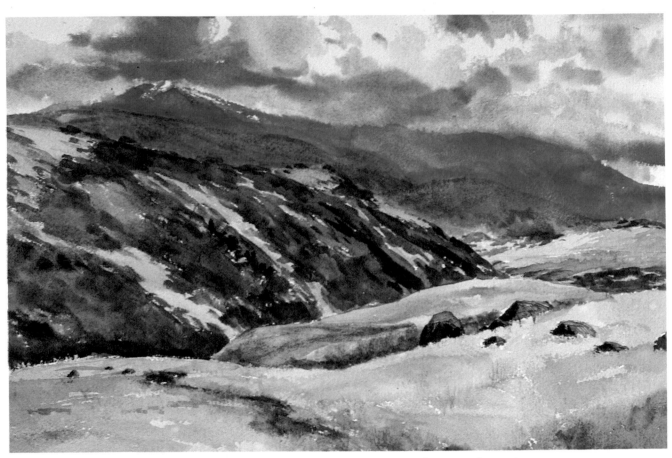

*High Meadows Above
Ashland*

13³/4 × 21¹/2 inches

*This Oregon painting makes use of a variety
of greens to portray grasses, some in
shadow, and scrub oaks on distant hills. It
also shows the blending of greens into the
blue of distant mountains.*

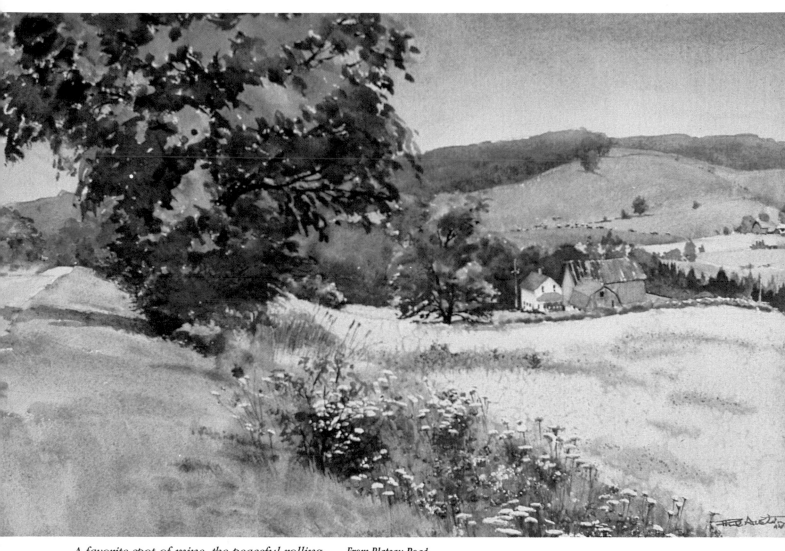

A favorite spot of mine, the peaceful rolling countryside of Door County, Wisconsin, where I live.

From Plateau Road
13³/₄ × 21¹/₂ inches

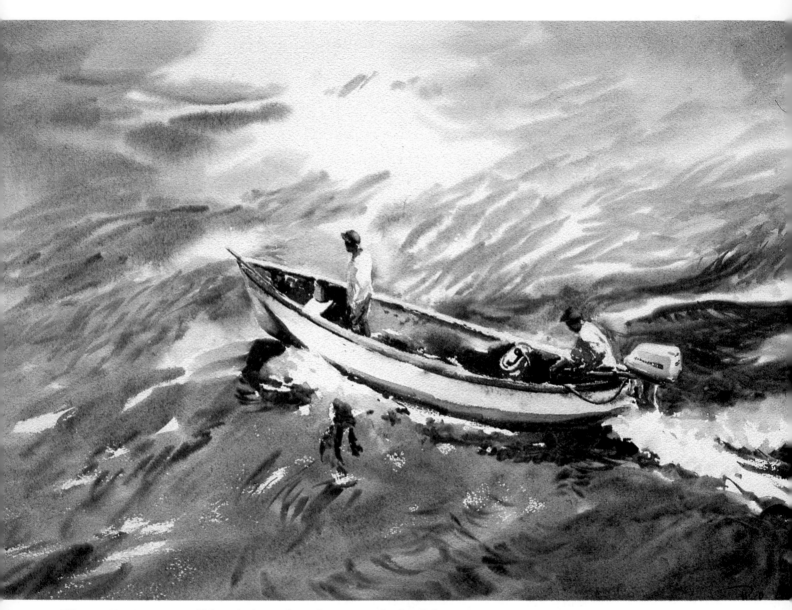

Fishermen, Mazatlan
21 × 29 inches
Collection of Mrs. Phil Austin

This painting—done from some lucky slides taken from the deck of a ferry in Mexico— took considerable planning, but very rapid painting of the water to give it movement. Lost and found edges on the boat and figures tie it all together.

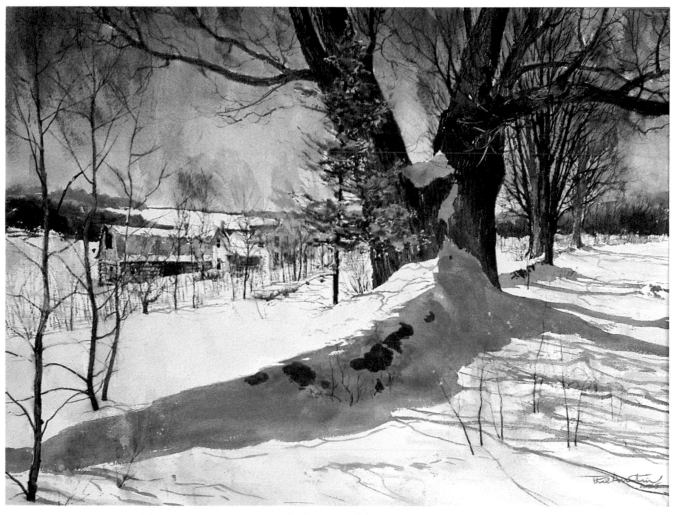

This painting is composed of many of the
things that make the Door County area
what it is. Sturdy old maples, stone walls
with snow wrapped about them, pine trees,
old farm houses, log barns, rolling
countryside with blue on distant ridges. I
used the rather dramatic shadow to put the
scene in deep winter, using a rather intense
cerulean and ultramarine mixture. The
barn and house were done with soft grays.
The middle distant trees were blurred into
the warm sky, which was mostly cerulean
with some cadmium yellow pale added
where the nearer tree limbs blurred into it.

Door County Winter
21½ × 29 inches
Collection of Northwest
Mutual Life Ins. Co.

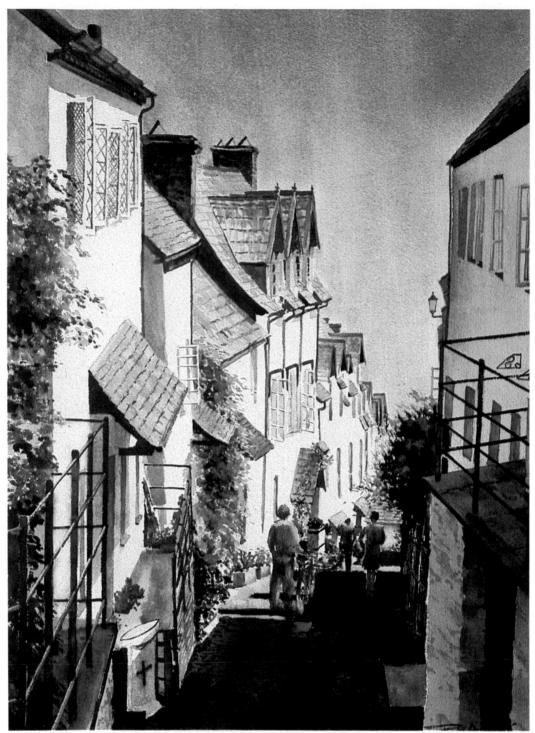

Several things were used to create this descending perspective. Careful drawing of the buildings helped, and was reinforced by the use of figures at different levels. Strong darks and areas of contrast also helped. The deep blue sky at the top strengthened the feeling of distant sky lower in the painting.

Down Into Clovelly, North Devon, England
29 × 21 inches
Collection of Mr. and Mrs. Gordon Bent

Index